Highlights

Michael Newman

Highlights

To everyone, thanks

Highlights
ISBN 978 1 76109 535 1
Copyright © text Michael Newman 2023

First published 2023 by
GINNINDERRA PRESS
PO Box 3461 Port Adelaide 5015
www.ginninderrapress.com.au

Contents

A short introduction, and a couple of warnings:	9
1940s	**11**
Hurricanes over the Pacific	13
Brushes with royalty	16
Nearly immolating my sister	18
Putting Mrs Jenkins in her place in Nuku'alofa	21
Delirium tremens	24
Turning the lights on in Queanbeyan	26
Sunday lunch in a Methodist parsonage	29
1950s	**33**
Cramming at Sydney Uni	35
A poem	36
1960s	**39**
A painting	41
Revealing next to all in Sydney	43
Qualifying my leads in Sydney	46
Justice in a suburban coroner's court	48
Flying a car in Pakistan	50
Talking of murder	54
Risking life and limb in London	57
Telling the world's longest joke in Covent Garden	60
Falling in love	64
Making arrangements in Versailles	67
A brush with revolution in Paris	70
Signing the marriage contract	75
Divine anger in Paris	77

Servant and master in Brittany	79
The perils of drink in the south of France	82

1970s   87

Rock Concerts in London and Saint Tropez	89
Childbirth in London	93
Testing parental love in Notting Hill Gate	98
An ecumenical baptism in the village of Rocbaron	101
Cross-cultural table manners	105
Contributing to international goodwill	106
Up against the authority in inner London	108
On a beach at Rye	113
A mural in a Shepherd's Bush basement	116
Dressmaking against racism in Shepherd's Bush	119

1980s   121

Unnoticed in Hanwell	123
Averting disaster in London	126
Wooden birds in the south of France	129
Telling the truth in le midi	131
Fire in London	134
A humdinger of a lowlight	139
Risking all in Wodonga	141
Lunch with my sister-in-law in le Marais	145
Brothers-in-law in Paris	150
On love, on love	155

1990s   159

The great disappearing act on Oxford Street, Sydney	161
Bringing the state of Victoria to a halt	163
Grind and the silver cowboy in Texas	166
Getting it wrong in Dallas	168
A tempest in New York	171
Forgetting Dallas	173
On a clothing workers' strike in Johannesburg	175

Alone in a Sharpeville shebeen	179
Spending social capital in Jo'burg	181
Farewelling my father-in-law	183
Circus in Laurieton	188
Wild weather over Dorrigo	193
Boff!	195
Accosted in Kingston, Jamaica	197
Seeing the sights in Jamaica	201
A multicultural send-off	203
Meeting a good person in South Africa	208
No need for dismay in Khayelitsha	210
A traveller's tale from Geneva	213
A small matter in Bangkok	216

2000s — 219

Understanding Noah	221
Warned in South Africa	224
From the valley of a thousand hills	226
Weeping for South Africa	228
A walk in the park	229
Soul dancing in Hobart	232
A moment to remember in a Sydney clinic	234
A drawing in Albi	236

2010s — 239

Enlightenment at Saint-Benoît-sur-Loire	241
Cross-cultural miscommunication in le Périgord	243
Drag night in Honolulu	247
An old flame in a moral philosophy class in Sydney	250
Finding the right word in a Sydney pub, and other fragments	252
The musings of a doting grandfather	257
Time well spent with a friend in Sydney	259
Chaos in Coledale	261
The dark art of labelling	264

Old Friends	270
A very short love poem	273
Postscript	275

A short introduction, and a couple of warnings:

First, the introduction: I have structured this book by looking back over my life, selecting the interesting bits and leaving out the humdrum that fills the spaces in between. Hence the title *Highlights*. Occasionally, I give in to the temptation to explain and/or analyse but you can move on to the next highlight as soon as you like.

And now to the warnings.

Looking back over my life brings me quickly to the question of veracity. The memories of a man in his eighties may not always be super accurate, but I have avoided giving the impression of uncertainty in the text. If I cannot remember whether something happened in 1961 or 1962, I plump for one of the two dates and state it as if I were certain. I recall conversations that I held with people as long ago as 1945 and write them down as if I have total recall, which I do not. The book you are about to read, then, is full of minor fabrications. But I make the following promise: the essence of every story is true.

Something of the same has to be said of my command of French. A number of highlights take place in France. I get by in French, but am not always as glibly fluent as I portray. However, there seems little point in presenting my side of conversations in a French filled with 'ums' and 'ahs' while I search for the right word, or try to get a pesky subjunctive right. Better that I translate my fractured French into reasonably fluent English, and get on with the story.

1940s

Hurricanes over the Pacific

In the early morning of Sunday, 7 December 1941, the Japanese entered the Second World War by mounting a massive surprise attack from both sea and air on the US naval base at Pearl Harbor, Hawaii. They damaged or sank four battleships, three cruisers, three destroyers, and a number of other ships, destroyed 188 aircraft, killed 2,403 people, and injured another 1,178.

My father – Eben Vickery Newman – was the Methodist minister in Tenterfield, a country town in the north of the state of New South Wales, Australia, at the time of the attack. People flocked to the morning service at Dad's church, seeking reassurance, I imagine, that the Lord would protect them; and it was at this inappropriate moment that my politically inept father felt he had to tell the congregation he was a pacifist.

Dad's prospects within the church suffered. He had been slated as the next principal of a theological college in Sydney but that was suddenly closed to him, and a missionary appointment, as principal of a boys' college in the kingdom of Tonga, became his only option. Tonga is a group of islands in the South Pacific eight hundred kilometres east of Fiji,

Our family lived for several weeks in a boarding house in Sydney, waiting for places on a flying boat to Auckland, New Zealand. We kept being bumped off to make way for military personnel. And we spent several weeks in another boarding house in Auckland, waiting for berths on the cargo boat that would take us to Tonga. Finally we boarded the boat, cleared the harbour and headed into the Pacific.

One of my earliest memories, if not the earliest, is of standing beside my mother on the rear deck of the cargo boat, surrounded on all sides by the Pacific Ocean. It was early 1943, and we were midway through the Second World War. There was an anti-aircraft gun on the rear deck, and every day at three p.m. the crew would assemble, ready the gun and mimic using it. Ammunition was limited and so they did not fire the thing. Our family, that is, my mum and dad, my sister and brother, and me, would assemble wearing our life jackets, and watch.

The Battle of the Coral Sea and the Battle of Midway may have happened and the Japanese navy may have been mauled, but submarines were still said to be active in the area. The boat's engine broke down twice, and each time we wallowed for hours while the crew fixed it.

On one of these occasions, one of the crew said cheerfully to my mother, 'And here we are, a sitting duck for any Jap sub that might come along.'

I can remember holding my mother's hand and feeling her fear as she said, 'Let's go below.'

Three days out from Nuku'alofa, the capital of Tonga, a Hurricane airplane appeared in the sky above us and circled the boat for a time, before heading away. There was, we were told, an air force base on the main island of Tonga Tabu. Two days out, and a succession of Hurricanes circled us for the better part of the day. One day out, and the planes circled us from first light until nightfall. I have another vivid memory, and that is of a Hurricane flying low over the boat and the pilot waving to us. On the following day, our cargo boat reached Nuku'alofa, and we went ashore.

We were greeted and housed for the first few days by the minister of the Methodist church in Nuku'alofa.

Over dinner on the first evening, my father mentioned the planes that had circled the boat for the past three days. It had been, he said, a great comfort to feel protected like that. 'They must have known that there was a minister and his family aboard,' he said.

His colleague looked dumbfounded for a moment, and then burst out laughing. 'They weren't looking after you,' he said. 'The boat was carrying a supply of whisky for their officers' mess. They weren't going to let the Japanese torpedo that.'

Most of the islands that make up the kingdom of Tonga are coral atolls, but there are some in the Vava'u group that are volcanic. On our first night on dry land, a Vava'u volcano grumbled a bit, and the quakes were felt in Nuku'alofa. I remember lying between my mum and dad while the house shook. Mum and Dad must have thought the planet was laughing at them.

Brushes with royalty

I have had two brushes with royalty, both of them when I was an infant in Tonga.

My mother – Ena Newman Smith – felt terribly isolated there. She was well read, had a restless, inquiring mind, and thrived on debate. In the 1940s, formal education for most Tongans finished at the end of primary school. Amongst the expatriates, there were few avid readers. And we lived some six kilometres out of Nuku'alofa, which made Mum's isolation physical as well as intellectual.

There was another educated and strongly independent woman on the islands, and that was Queen Salote, the reigning monarch. She had travelled, gone to university in New Zealand, read widely and, in all probability, felt the same sense of intellectual isolation as my mother. She contacted Mum and invited her to afternoon tea. This had to be done discreetly. Mum was a commoner, and a foreigner, and it would not do for the queen to be seen spending more than a limited amount of time with her.

My mother would take a horse-drawn sulky into Nuku'alofa, go to the palace (a large two-storey weatherboard house on the waterfront), enter by a side door, and have tea with the queen. Sometimes, my mother would take me with her, and the queen would dandle me on her knee. Do I have memories of this? Well, yes, I do.

My second brush with royalty was a life or death matter. I was five, and at a beach picnic with the rest of our family and some twenty or so others. The beach was fine yellow-white sand. The water covered a flat shelf of brown coral and was only a few centimetres in depth. Dotted here and there in the coral were holes, some of them deep. They had sand at the bottom, and were an alluring blue-green.

If we wore our sandals, we kids could splash about on the coral shelf. Of course I had been warned not to go into the holes. And of course, in one of those impossible, inevitable moments, when every single adult happened to be looking elsewhere, I stepped into a hole. I went down, and in a classic process of drowning, came up only to gasp, struggle and go down again. I came up the second time, gasped, gurgled and went down again. On my third time coming up, a hand grabbed me under my armpit and lifted me up out of the water. I did not know, of course, but the hand belonged to the massive figure of the heir apparent of the kingdom of Tonga.

As royalty must do all the time, he had lost interest in whatever was attracting the attention of all the other picnic-goers, and turned his gaze seaward at the moment I came up for the third time. In a couple of strides he was there and stopped me going down for a fourth, and conceivably last, time.

Now there he was, standing on the coral shelf, and holding me aloft. My parents, my sister and brother, and the rest of the picnic-goers were standing on the beach, open-mouthed. I expelled the water remaining in my lungs and resumed regular breathing by screaming my head off.

Nearly immolating my sister

Our house at Tupou College in Tonga was a three-bedroom weatherboard bungalow. My brother Sandy and I had to share a bedroom, but our big sister Yo (short for Yolande), had a bedroom of her own, with French windows opening onto a wide veranda. At the time I was four, Sandy was six, and Yo was nine. We all slept with mosquito nets attached to hooks in the ceilings and hanging down around our beds. In those days, mosquito nets were flammable.

Early one morning in March 1944, Sandy, our brother, carried a lighted candle into Yo's bedroom. He intended waking Yo up and singing 'happy birthday'. I was tagging along behind him. Yo sat up on her bed, smiling and hugging her knees. Sandy tried to part the mosquito net with his free hand, so that he and I could climb onto the bed beside her.

And the inevitable happened.

The flame of the candle licked the edge of the net, and in one gigantic whoosh the net burnt. Sandy fell backwards, knocking me out of harm's way. Yo sat surrounded for an instant by a wall of flame. And then it was over, the sudden silence after that terrifying whoosh marked by wisps of blackened net floating in the air.

The silence was short-lived. Yo screamed, I screamed, and Sandy ran onto the front veranda shouting, 'Yo's bed's on fire! Yo's bed's on fire!'

Tupou College grew a lot of its own food. To the side of the house there was a lawn and beyond that a vegetable garden. Three college students, aged fifteen or sixteen, were at work there.

They heard Sandy's call and came running, leapt onto the veranda, raced into Yo's bedroom, and began taking the bed out of the house. Yo was still sitting on the bed but she was thrown forward as it collided with the French window, one side of which was closed. The three young men dragged the bed back, so that they could open the other side of the French window, and tried again. There was a lot of movement and a lot of noise.

Having created the problem, Sandy tried to put things right by shouting, 'The bed's not on fire. The bed's not on fire.'

But the young men were shouting instructions at each other, and did not hear him. Now they were tipping the bed and Yo began slipping off. Somehow, she hung on as the bed was dragged onto the veranda. Mum and Dad raced into the room, followed by a wonderful woman called Melino Faibola, who walked across the room and stopped the young men from throwing the bed and my sister off the veranda. Everyone calmed down.

I got lots of hugs because I was the youngest. Yo got lots of hugs because she had been through a near-death experience. And Sandy got a telling off…

Years later – that is, six plus decades later – we three siblings enjoyed a well-watered dinner together and did some serious reminiscing. As the evening progressed, it was clear that Sandy was still smarting from what he perceived as our parents' unfair treatment of him. He seemed to have extended that moment in Tonga into the rest of his childhood and formed the idea that he was not loved as much as Yo and I were. Yo and I talked about this later. Apart from the brief moment when Sandy came close to immolating her, burning our weatherboard house down and leaving us homeless on a south Pacific island isolated from the rest of the world by war, neither of us could think of any other occasion when our parents did not treat, and love, the three of us equally.

Yo says my account of her near immolation concurs more or less with her memory of the event, but that she is pretty sure it was not her birthday, and that our much loved, much missed, often misled brother had in all probability got the date wrong. Perhaps, because he did get things wrong from time to time, he exasperated our parents more than Yo and I did, and he mistook that exasperation for a lack of love.

I have tried to make light of it but, having written the above, I sense that I may be painting Sandy as a tragic figure. Again I consulted Yo, and she said, 'Perhaps he was.'

Putting Mrs Jenkins in her place in Nuku'alofa

I want to talk about Jesus. But wait, wait! I am not going to try to convert you. I am a person of an unshakably secular disposition, but I like Jesus, or the image I have of the man.

Early in his ministry, Jesus took to the road, which is a tough life. Within a week or two, his hair would have become a tangled mess, his clothes would have been filthy, and he would have smelled pretty rank. The image we get from stained-glass windows of a gentle, wafty kind of figure with recently shampooed hair and very clean robes has got to be wrong. And yet, if the gospels are anything to go by, people ignored his bedraggled state.

Jesus was a talker, and his voice would have been permanently hoarse, like a jazz singer, or a heavy smoker. But he would have kept a good bit in reserve for the big open-air events like the Sermon on the Mount, when he needed a voice like a foghorn. And then there were his eyes. To hold the attention of the people in the back rows, he must have had that penetrating gaze which gave the impression that he was talking individually to each and every person in the crowd.

And Jesus did not just talk. He wove stories with moral or philosophical conundrums in them that left his listeners thinking. Of course, like every inveterate storyteller, he could go over the top, as he did in the story of the prodigal son. No one, but no one in this wide world of ours would have killed the fatted calf without getting the little bastard to do more than simply beg for forgiveness. I would have had him cleaning out the sheds, and out in the fields for three months at least before organising any kind of event welcoming him home. Even then, I would have made the event low-key just in case the kid took off again.

Jesus seduced people into following him. He could convince the sick that they were cured. In the case of people with psychosomatic and stress-related illnesses, that may have been true. And he was street smart. He travelled light and probably had little or no cash, but he always seemed to know how to wangle a decent meal, and get somewhere to sleep.

I also liked Jesus because he was a tradie (tradesman, for non-Australian speakers), having done his apprenticeship in carpentry before taking to the road. Obviously, I have come up with this image since I became an adult, but I already had an affection for the man when I was five or six and our family was still living in Tonga. And it is natural that I would, because I heard my father talk engagingly about him on Sunday mornings in the large thatched chapel of Tupou College, where Dad was principal and where our family lived. My warts-and-all image derives from my gentle theologian father's constant efforts to make Jesus real to his listeners.

During our time in Tonga, we were inevitably drawn into the social life of the expatriates living there. These were the people who managed the general store in Nuku'alofa, the other Methodist minister and his family, the couple who ran the boarding house, and a handful of public servants who were working for the Tongan government.

All this was another day and another age, and the group was unashamedly and/or unthinkingly racist. Even though the majority of the expats came from New Zealand and Australia, people in the group called themselves Europeans, which was a euphemism for 'white'. The island's doctor was ostracised, not just because he drank heavily but because he had a Tongan wife and so, in the racist term of the time, had 'gone native'. And there were enough of us white kids for a European school to be set up, which was open to any white child, but only to privileged or super bright Tongans. Worst of all, expats tended to address Tongans by their first names, infantilising the lot of them.

'Good morning, Mr Johnson.'

'Good morning, Malachi.'

The self-appointed social doyenne of the Europeans was Mrs Jenkins, and she held afternoon tea parties for women expats, to which children could be brought. The kids played and were fed in one room, and the grown-ups drank their tea in the next. I came to hate Mrs Jenkins after she stood over me and made me eat the small remaining pieces of red jelly on my plate.

On another of these afternoons, Mrs Jenkins instituted the most appalling inquisition. We children were called into the grown-ups' room one by one and had to stand there answering questions put to us by the dreadful person herself. I was called in and duly asked about school (which I was starting next year), what my brother and I did on the weekends, and so on. Then we came to the big question.

'And tell me, Michael. What are you going to be when you grow up?'

'A carpenter,' I said without any hesitation.

'Oh, Michael,' Mrs Jenkins said. 'Carpenters are common people. Don't you want to be something more respectable, like a lawyer or a doctor or an officer in the army?'

'Jesus Christ was a carpenter,' I said in the bell-like tones of the small and innocent child.

My mother and I left the tea party soon after that.

Delirium tremens

It was late 1945. I was nearly six. We were still in Tonga. And Dad was away (and out of touch) for a fortnight on the island of Vav'au, the second largest island in the scatter of islands that made up the kingdom of Tonga.

The pain started late in the afternoon. Mum tried to comfort me but without success. My whimpers gave way to screams and Mum ran out of the house and across the college campus to the senior students' classroom. There she asked them to organise a horse, sulky and driver to take us into Nuku'alofa.

Our driver drove as quickly as the unsurfaced road allowed, and pulled up outside the house of the only doctor on the island. Mum carried me in. Here things slowed a little. The doctor seemed unsure of himself. He prodded my stomach and I screamed some more. The doctor opined that I had acute appendicitis. Mum asked him if he could help.

'Don't go back to the college this evening,' the doctor said. 'Stay at the guest house. I will meet you there first thing tomorrow morning. I should be all right by then.'

'What does that mean?' Mum asked him.

'I've had a couple of drinks.'

We drove down the main street to the waterfront and I stopped screaming. Floating two or three hundred metres beyond the reef was a British warship, sleek, powerful, grey, giving off a hum of activity that was punctuated by occasional clanking noises.

We checked into the guesthouse and I cried throughout the night. The only other guests were a married couple who had come to bolster Tonga's civil service. God knows what they thought of their first night in the kingdom.

In the morning, two things happened. The islands' doctor arrived, and Mum disappeared. She fled the guesthouse and headed for the palace, where she abandoned all palace protocol, and shouted and wept and beat her fists on the palace door like a mad thing.

No one came to the palace door, but things did begin happening. A group of men assembled on the beach below the palace. They ran a boat down to the water, climbed in and began rowing towards the warship. They carried a letter of welcome from Queen Salote and a note asking the ship's captain to do what he could for me. Four of the palace staff were dispatched to the island's two-bed hospital to give it a thorough cleaning. A nurse with years of experience within the New Zealand health service was found. She began sterilising a meagre collection of instruments, and preparing one of the two rooms as the operating theatre. The rowers headed back to land, carrying the ship's senior surgeon with them.

When the surgeon arrived at the hospital, he spoke briefly to the islands' doctor, thanked him for his speedy diagnosis, and said there was no need for him to stay on. The doctor left.

The surgeon had looked dismayed when he entered the island's hospital, but now he said to the nurse, 'Shall we make a start?'

The nurse nodded.

That then is how I had my appendix removed by a renowned Scots surgeon in the middle of the Pacific Ocean in the middle of a world war.

I woke from the operation to find that I was sharing the hospital with one other patient. He was a huge man in his early fifties. For the main part, he was cheerful, but there were moments when he would shout out in alarm, clutch at his body, and cover his eyes with his forearms. Years later, Dad explained that my fellow patient had been in the midst of a battle with alcoholism and had been experiencing withdrawal symptoms known as delirium tremens.

'The symptoms can take the form of terrifying hallucinations,' Dad said, and went on, 'That's right. No one thought to tell us.'

Turning the lights on in Queanbeyan

We came back from Tonga to Australia in mid-1947. Dad was asked to put a faltering Sydney girls' school to rights, which he did (and for which he received little or no thanks), and in 1948 he was appointed as the Methodist minister in Queanbeyan, a country town on the southern tablelands of New South Wales.

Queanbeyan was not considered a prize appointment, and I remember a sallow, quietly spoken minister from the Congregational Church coming to our house one evening in the weeks before we made the move. He and Dad locked themselves away in Dad's study and, as I learnt years later, the Congregational minister urged Dad to quit the Methodists and join the Congregationalists. Dad chose to stay in the Methodist Church and confront, if needs be, a mixture of insult and ostracism from a group of his peers who continued to condemn him for his pacifism (and, Mum explained to me once, for wearing his hair just a bit too long, and a jacket and trousers instead of a suit!).

I was eight when we arrived in Queanbeyan and twelve when we left. They were golden years for country town kids. We ran in a gang, rode our bikes along back roads and fire breaks, climbed the nearby hills, jumped from the suspension bridge into the river, and tried smoking a very cheap and horrid cigarette appropriately called Turf. In the river, you had to keep moving to avoid the leeches, and the cigarettes were useful, if only to burn off the leeches that did manage to lock on to you.

We did not have electricity when we moved into the parsonage. Mum cooked on a cast-iron range, stoking the fire with wood that Dad chopped late each afternoon. She washed our clothes and the bed linen in a copper filled with soapy water brought to the boil over a fire, and she wrung out the washing using a mangle. We had a meat safe hanging in the shade on the back veranda, and an icebox housing the block of ice delivered weekly by the ice man who, like the milkman, drove a horse and cart. On Saturday evenings, Dad would use a shovel to get hot coals from the range, and he would walk, holding the shovel out in front of him, along the hallway to the bathroom, where he would use the coals to get the chip heater going for Yo, Sandy and me to have our baths.

For lighting, we used a number of hurricane lamps and two pressure lamps. The hurricane lamps produced a soft yellow light, and the pressure lamps produced a bright white light. Each evening, Dad would light the lamps. This involved topping up the kerosene in each lamp, checking and trimming the wicks, and pumping up the pressure in the pressure lamps. He would then light the hurricane lamps, and last of all the two pressure lamps.

Electricity came to our house in 1951, and was one of the many changes in everyone's lives resulting from the wool boom. Two men worked for a couple of days, bringing the electricity in from the street to our house, and installing electric lamps that hung from the ceiling in every room, and power points for the oven and refrigerator in the kitchen.

Dad must have been away because, on the day the electricity was connected, he came into the house late in the afternoon, put all the lamps on the kitchen table, and began his ritual of preparing to light them. Mum came and fetched us kids, putting her finger to her mouth. We tiptoed down the hallway, and assembled at the kitchen door. Dad went on preparing the lamps, and just as he was about to light the first one, Mum flicked the switch next to the door and the new electric light hanging from the ceiling came on. Dad stopped, looked up in momentary surprise, and then turned and looked at Mum with a smile. It is nice to witness an unguarded moment of communication between people who love one another.

We kids ran around the table chanting, 'We've got electric light, we've got electric light.'

Mum and Dad stood looking at each other a little longer. Queanbeyan, belatedly, had entered the twentieth century.

In Australian country towns, the First World War, then the Depression and then the Second World War put a stop to development, so that, in 1950, people were living with a technology that was unchanged from the end of the nineteenth century. All of which means that my style of life would have been much the same as that of a boy my age in 1900.

I imagine seeing him on the other side of our street, and waving to him.

Sunday lunch in a Methodist parsonage

My father may have been a Methodist minister but that did not stop my mother being an atheist. They loved each other, of that there was no doubt. You could see it in the way they looked at each other. But they did have radically different views about religion, and life, and what everything was all about.

Mum's mother had died in childbirth, and her father had abandoned her shortly after that. Mum was brought up by a collection of aunts, whose chaotic and sometimes penurious help stopped abruptly when she graduated (with a first class honours degree) from the University of Melbourne in 1919. Mum became a teacher, and worked her way up to the post of deputy principal of one of the largest girls' schools in Sydney. She married Dad in 1934, when she was thirty-five, and they left soon after the wedding for two years in England, where Dad completed a degree at Oxford.

When Mum and Dad married, Mum kept her atheism to herself in the (entirely correct) belief that some of Dad's colleagues and a good number of the congregation in Dad's church would not understand. This led to some anomalies. For example, the minister's wife was expected to play an active role alongside her husband in the affairs of the circuit (Methodist for parish). One of these was to be the chairperson of the local branch of the Ladies' Church Aid Association, which in turn required her to end the meetings with an extempore prayer. Through the years, and in each of the circuits to which Dad was sent, mother ended the meetings of the Ladies' Church Aid Associations with humanist perorations extolling the ethical life.

No one in all those years noticed (or if they did, they shut up about it) that she never made mention of God or the Lord or Christ, the

Saviour. She did end her perorations with a firm Amen, and everyone seemed satisfied with that.

On Sundays, Mum would take us kids across the paddock between the parsonage (Methodist for vicarage) and the weatherboard Methodist church for the eleven o'clock service. We would sit in the minister's family pew. Dad would officiate and deliver his sermon. He was fastidious in keeping his sermons to fifteen minutes or less, but that still seemed a long time to me. At the end of the service, Mum would take us back to the house. Dad had to stand at the church door and shake people's hands and chat, so he would come back to the house half-an-hour or so later. We would sit at the table, and Mother would take the Sunday roast out of the oven and put it in front of Dad. He would carve, and place slices of meat on our plates. Mum would serve the vegetables and pour the gravy. Once we all had our plates in front of us, Dad would put the carving knife and fork aside, and say grace.

And when grace was finished, Mum would say. 'Now, in your sermon this morning you said…' and their endless argument would be resumed. Yo on one side of the table and Sandy and me on the other side would look from one parent to the other, a bit like people watching a tennis match.

Dad, in his quiet and sometimes infuriating way, could strike back. It was 1957, and we had left the bush to live in Sydney. We had just got a television set, and Dad, Mum, Sandy, Yo and I were watching. It was Easter, and on the screen Christ was labouring up the hill carrying a massive wooden cross. Dad had fallen asleep. Mum was shifting in her seat. Suddenly she leant over, and shook Dad awake. He looked at her.

'Listen,' Mum said, 'without any of your theological claptrap, do you or do you not believe in the bodily resurrection?'

My father was a believer, but he was also a heretic. 'No,' he said and went back to sleep.

My mother died in a car accident in late 1968. I was living in London at the time and could not get back to Sydney in time for the funeral. In those days, you were still required to have various vaccinations, some of which took too long before they were deemed effective. Dad wrote a long letter to me after the funeral. A number of his colleagues had been tumbling over each other to preside or contribute in some way at the funeral service. Dad said he had been obliged to take each of them aside and explain that 'Your mother was not a conventional Christian', and to ask them to avoid phrases such as 'Ena has come to rest in the bosom of the Lord'.

A lesser man might have been tempted to reclaim her as a member of the holy flock, now that she was unable to speak for herself, but not my dad.

1950s

Cramming at Sydney Uni

I was a student at the University of Sydney from 1958 to 1961. I was enrolled in the Faculty of Arts, and majored in English literature. I got involved early on in student theatre and in the student newspaper *Honi Soit*, and, because of these extracurricular activities, I did not attend many lectures. I managed to pass each year by borrowing friends' lecture notes and using a drug that I acquired from a morally challenged pharmacist with a shop in an adjoining suburb.

The drug enabled me to go without sleep and to absorb just enough information to get by in the exams. I was not the only person patronising the pharmacist, and I like to think he retired early and spent the rest of a long and agreeable life in tropical climes. Without his help, I would not have got the undistinguished BA that I did.

In one of the exam papers, I began to feel drowsy, and so I fished out my little tin case holding the miracle drug. There was a small round hole in the corner of the tin case, and you had to tap the tin to make a single tablet fall out on to the palm of your other hand. This I did, but the tablet missed my hand and rolled down the examination hall between two lines of desks occupied by fellow examinees. I slipped out of my seat and crawled along the floor and retrieved the tablet, all under the eye of an invigilator who chose to do nothing. I assume any other action would have involved her in too much paperwork.

A poem

When I was cramming for an English exam in 1959 I came across this poem by Wallace Stevens:

> Call the roller of big cigars,
> The muscular one, and bid him whip
> In kitchen cups concupiscent curds.
> Let the wenches dawdle in such dress
> As they are used to wear, and let the boys
> Bring flowers in last month's newspapers.
> Let be be finale of seem.
> The only emperor is the emperor of ice cream.
>
> Take from the dresser of deal,
> Lacking the three glass knobs, that sheet
> On which she embroidered fantails once
> And spread it so as to cover her face.
> If her horny feet protrude, they come
> To show how cold she is, and dumb.
> Let the lamp affix its beam.
> The only emperor is the emperor of ice cream.

I had to hasten on with my cramming, but I went back to the poem when the exams were over. I can count the poems I really like on the fingers of one hand: W.H. Auden's 'September, 1939', Gerard Manly Hopkins' 'The Windhover', Andrew Marvell's 'To his coy mistress', John Donne's 'Busy old fool, unruly sun', and, up front, Wallace Stevens' 'The emperor of ice cream'. No surprises there.

The images in 'The emperor of ice cream' are dark and uncompromising: 'the roller of big cigars, the muscular one'. Just look at the size of him! And the women: 'Let the wenches dawdle in such dress as they are used to wear.' Here they come, slowly, provocatively. And the boys – the pimps – with flowers 'in last month's newspapers.' Theirs is a perfunctory gesture. The woman is dead. And if you have any doubts, then 'let the lamp affix its beam', and see 'how cold she is, and dumb'.

The woman's body will be buried along with 'that sheet on which she embroidered fantails once'. And when her one attempt at creating something beautiful has been taken away, all we will have left is the solipsistic act of eating ice cream.

Priorities change. There was a time when emperors (some at least) were people of substance, lovers of art, philosopher queens and philosopher kings. Now 'the only emperor is the emperor of ice cream'.

The poem was published amidst the growing din of the roaring twenties, and the rampant capitalism that went with them. Stevens is depicting a small and drab event taking place unnoticed just a street or two back from the bright lights of the big city. And he is depicting radical cultural change, in which the unholy pragmatist is replacing the artist as the person who interprets the world for us. 'Let be be finale of seem'. We have prostituted art. Let harsh, unfriendly reality be what's left after we have done away with imagination.

I am still moved by the poem, and amused by the commentaries I found when I googled the poem's title. Few acknowledged the sexual context of the poem, which is signalled early on by Stevens's use of the words 'concupiscent' and 'wenches', and made unambiguous in the image of a street walker's 'horny feet'. But then, most of the commentaries I found were directed at undergraduate students, and perhaps the commentators felt they should protect their charges for that little bit longer

1960s

A painting

Art galleries can be hard work. Often there are too many paintings or photos or installations in the one exhibition, and I leave the gallery glutted. Worst of all are those small rooms where you sit on benches in the dark and are subjected to shooshing noises, scrambled dialogue and flashing images.

Moments of inspiration are rare.

I looked at, really looked at, a painting for the first time when I was about twenty. The painting was in an exhibition of paintings by Ian Fairweather. I am not even sure that I had been to a gallery before this one, but I had read a review claiming that Fairweather was the best Australian painter alive, and I wanted to see what that might mean. I walked around the several rooms looking at painting after painting. All were scruffy disarrays of lines and shapes. Fairweather would use the white of the canvas or the sheet of paper he was painting on as a background, over which he would superimpose an untidy outline painted in broad brushstrokes. One painting had been given a whole wall to itself. The background was the white of the canvas or paper (I cannot remember which) and the shapes were outlined in a dark luminescent blue.

A man was standing, apparently entranced, in front of the painting, and I watched him instead of the painting. When he moved away, I assumed his place.

The painting was reasonably large and I was standing back from it. At first, it seemed completely without form, a striking mass of ragged lines. Then I began to see the lines as shapes arranged in rows, one row above the other. Now, the shapes assumed the outlines of people, and the whole painting began to give off the impression of a medieval frieze.

For a while, the impression held firm, then other lines began assuming shapes and I had the impression of more rows of figures behind as well. The painting took on an indeterminate depth, and after a while the sense of a frieze began to slip away. Now, the painting suggested the untidiness of the Australian bush, and the rows of figures seemed to be advancing, out of the bush. I, in my turn, stood entranced, learning for the first time that a painting can grow before the eyes, occupy its own time, create its own space and continually renew itself.

Years later, I was telling Roger, my French brother-in-law, about this experience. I told him that I did not understand why that one painting had such an impact on me, and others did not. He said that the seventeenth century French philosopher Blaise Pascal believed that each painting had a perfect place from which it could be viewed. The man in the gallery had found Pascal's perfect place and, without knowing he was doing it, had passed it on to me.

Revealing next to all in Sydney

Until the 1960s, Sydney was a dreary, conventional place. Shops closed on Saturday at noon, and nothing was open for the rest of the weekend. There was no organised sport on Sunday. About the only thing people did was go to church.

With the Christian religion came the age-old and ugly division between Protestants and Catholics, but I am pretty sure that both parties would have agreed that depicting the sexual act in public would ensure you a permanent spot in the fires of hell. As for actually committing the act in public…

I performed in two university revues, one in 1960 called *Nymphs and shepherds*, the other in 1961 called *Wet blankets*. The director of the 1960 revue was ahead of his time. He dressed the eight of us in the cast in leotards for the opening act. This caused some angst, because parading our bodies in quite that way was a new experience for some of us. Would the audience be shocked? And what kind of support should the men wear?

Midway through the show, there was a sketch retelling the story of Helen of Troy. Helen was dressed in a long flowing robe, and she stood on a trolley, which was controlled by ropes from the wings. The trolley passed from one side of the stage to the other regularly throughout the sketch, with Helen in different poses. I was on stage playing the part of Achilles (yes) and so had a close-up view of what followed.

Towards the end of the sketch, Paris mounted the trolley, took Helen in his arms, and the trolley trundled off stage. On one night, however, the trolley would not move. Helen and Paris were in each other's arms, smiling at the audience, and not moving. Their smiles became fixed, while the stagehands operating the trolley tried to make it move. This they did by tugging with increasing force on the ropes. The trolley moved, got stuck again, and Helen and Paris fell over.

Now, follow me carefully. Paris was wearing a small Trojan skirt, and it flipped up to show, to those of us close enough to see such unwelcome detail, that he was wearing a jock strap, which may have done its job of providing support, but left his backside uncovered. From the audience, it must have looked as if he were naked from the waist down. Helen had fallen under him, and her robe had been dragged up around her thighs. To this juncture, Helen might just have got away with it, but to gain purchase on the trolley and not roll off onto the stage, she raised both her knees.

Since both Helen and Paris were fighting to stay on the trolley, there was lots of body movement, and it looked for all the world as if they were enthusiastically engaging in what Kingsley Amis described in one of his novels as 'the ultimate indecency'.

The sketch, and this description of it, ends with a stagehand walking on stage and pushing the trolley off, to the wild applause and/or gasps of condemnation from the audience...

Some of our number in that revue became national, and even international, figures. The director was Leo Schofield, and he was just such a figure, a passionate advocate, commentator and columnist on opera and theatre, the director of arts festivals in Melbourne, Sydney, Hobart and Brisbane, food critic, and much, much more.

On stage were Mungo MacCallum, who became a member of the Canberra press gallery, a renowned writer, and eccentric public intellectual; John Elder, who became a leading eye surgeon; Colleen Chesterman, who became a prominent femocrat (feminist bureaucrat) holding senior positions in the NSW premier's department, the NSW Council of Social Services, the University of Technology, Sydney, and more; Anne Schofield, who became an influential figure in the growth and development of Sydney theatre, and an acknowledged expert on antique jewellery; Jill Kitson, who became a much loved broadcaster on ABC radio, devising and presenting programs on books, the quirks of the

English language, and Australian history; John Clifton-Bligh, who went on to join the British army and rose to the rank of colonel; Graham MacDonald, who became an internationally renowned renal specialist; Maggie Blinco, who went on to become a much loved working actor in the Sydney theatrical and TV scene; Jenny Towndrow, who became a distinguished publisher, and author; and Robyn Waterhouse, who co-wrote a book called *The ripples before the new wave* about this period of intense theatrical activity at the University of Sydney.

In the wings, literally and so to speak, were John Hoddinott, who trained as an aeronautical engineer, worked for some years in Milan, and then returned to Sydney knowing more about the digital world than anyone else, and David Spode, who was active in the university theatrical scene as a designer and director, went on to work as a designer for BBCTV, and became a well-known antiquarian bookseller.

And among the several people who wrote sketches for the revue was Clive James, who went on to become…well, Clive James.

And there you have it. I have laid myself open to attack by people I have not included and who believe that I should have, and I have laid myself open to even more furious attack from those I have included and who want nothing to do with this project.

Qualifying my leads in Sydney

In my final year at university, I co-edited *Honi Soit*, the student newspaper, and based on this experience, I was employed by the *Sydney Sun* in 1962 as a D-grade journalist. I lasted less than a year.

All the other journalists had worked as cadets. When they became D-grade journalists, they already had years of experience and knew what to do. I was paid more than the cadets, but had no experience and did not know what to do. There was no induction program and so I had to learn as I went along. It was like the nightmare that can visit actors, in which they find themselves in the wings and about to go on stage and they realise they have not learnt their lines.

Some of my journalist colleagues understood the dilemma I was in and gave me tips when they could. The main one was to qualify my lead. News stories all followed the same pattern. You wrote the lead sentence, which encapsulated the whole story:

A man shot dead his wife's lover when the lover came to their house late at night, Haberfield Magistrate's court was told today.

You then provided the details to clarify your lead:

The man is…(one initial, then family name, then occupation)
  The lover was…(one initial, then family name, then occupation, and make sure you got the tense right)
  The wife is …(one initial, then family name)
  The house is in (name of street and suburb, never house number)…
  The lover came to the house after 11.30 at night on (day of week, date).
  'He was drunk and shouting,' the defendant alleged.
  'I felt threatened,' he said…

And so it went. Each sentence was a separate paragraph, and you wrote the paragraphs in an order of decreasing importance. If there was not enough space on the page, the compositors could pull out the bottom paragraphs without having to read them, knowing that the basic facts of the story would remain intact.

I was on the staff of the *Sydney Sun*, but when I did court reporting, I would file an initial report from a phone box to the sister afternoon paper called the *Sun*, then head back to the office to type the story up and submit it to the copy editors for the next morning's edition of the *Herald*.

When the last edition of the *Sun* had been put to bed, Reg Halliday, the chief of staff of the *Sun*, was often very chatty. My desk was near his office and he would stroll out, sit down and talk.

'Y'know, Mike, I don't have much to do with the church these days, but last Sunday some friends were having a kiddy christened and my wife dragged me along. I hadn't realised it, but we had to stay for the whole service, and I had to listen to the minister preaching his sermon. All the way through, I wanted to stand up and shout, "Qualify your lead, you bastard!"'

PS: My co-editor of *Honi Soit*, David Solomon, was in reality the editor. I wrote a weekly column and edited the arts page and not much more. I wandered off to enjoy the 1960s in London while David stayed put in Australia and became a highly respected professional in his field. Among other things, he was political correspondent to the *Australian*, president of the Canberra Press Gallery, press secretary to Prime Minister Gough Whitlam, and contributing editor of the *Courier Mail* in Brisbane. David studied law, wrote books, and wrote and published a newsletter called the *Legal Reporter*, in which he reported on matters before the High Court.

Justice in a suburban coroner's court

There were memorable moments in my year as a journalist.

I was a passenger in the back seat of a press car in high-speed pursuit of two police cars in high-speed pursuit of a fleeing crook, all before compulsory seat belts.

I wrote up the story of a train driver who mixed a cough mixture so potent that he missed a station, and then made an unscheduled stop halfway along the platform of the next. Passengers toppled out of the train and on to the platform in some distress. Others raced through the train to a point where they could topple out on to the platform in some distress.

And I witnessed a police prosecutor and a magistrate in a suburban coroner's court tie up proceedings to such an extent that the miserable woman in the dock, who had been charged with infanticide, might be cared for and never called back to the court.

The court was a coroner's court but there was a stage in proceedings when the coroner reconvened the court as a magistrate's court in order to charge the defendant and set a date for a trial. The defendant was duly charged, but no date was set.

The magistrate went on, 'How should we proceed, sergeant?'

'We will need a full report, your worship.'

'I would want a thorough job done, sergeant.'

'That might take a while, your worship.'

'Not our problem, sergeant. Let the professionals take their time. Do we need to set a date to return to court?'

'I don't see how we can, your worship.'

'So be it,' said the magistrate. 'Do you have that?' This was directed at the clerk of the court, who, face impassive, recorded the ruling (or whatever else you might call it) in a clatter of rapid typing. 'And make sure you have the phrase "a full psychiatric report" in there somewhere,' the magistrate said.

'Already done,' the clerk said.

Magistrates rarely talked to reporters, but this one did. 'How,' he asked me as we fell into step on our way out of the building, 'would custody help anyone like that?'

I grew to dislike my job intensely. I reported the gruesome details of a murder as recounted in the Sydney Coroners Court, and saw my handiwork appear the next morning under the headline:

'Dizzy spells' claim: Hammer killing alleged.

Enough. In those convention-ridden days of the early 1960s, the only way a middle-class boy could leave a job without shaming his family was to go overseas.

I went overseas.

Flying a car in Pakistan

In early 1963, Mungo MacCallum, David Spode and I drove from Sydney to Athens. Not literally, of course. We loaded a car onto a liner at Sydney and offloaded it at Colombo. From there, we drove to the northern tip of what was Ceylon and is now Sri Lanka, loaded the car on to a boat there, offloaded it at the southernmost tip of India and drove overland from there. We went to amazing places – Madurai, Madras, Belur, Halebid, Bangalore, Agra, New Delhi, Jaipur, Amritsar, the far north of Pakistan near the Afghan border, across the Quetta desert and into Iran, Isfahan, Teheran, into Turkey, Erzurum, Istanbul, Thessaloniki, and finally Athens.

We were in a remote part of north Pakistan, driving down the side of a mountain range on a dirt road full of hairpin bends, and I was at the wheel. As we twisted and turned, we caught glimpses of the valley floor, which looked as flat as a tabletop, and of our road, which ran across the valley in a straight line to the foot of another mountain range. It was afternoon. The road over the pass had slowed us down, and we were anxious about the time. Our map showed that we still had a long way to go to get to the village that was our destination for the night. Driving during the day was hard enough. The road was often not much more than two tyre tracks, and from time to time we had to negotiate small sand drifts. (We had mats for that.) Driving in the dark would be hazardous. If we drove off the road, we could get lost.

I sped up as we hit the dead straight road on the valley floor, not just because we had to make up for lost time, but as a release from driving at a crawl for the past two hours. I relaxed. The four windows were open, and the hot air rushed through the car, ruffling our hair. All was well.

For no reason that I could discern, there was a mound in the middle of the valley, and the road went up one side of it and down the other. I was still at the wheel and I admit that I simply did not see the mound. It was a brownish-yellow, like the rest of our surroundings. We went up our side of the mound at full speed and then the car was airborne. There was the whine of the engine as the wheels were released from the grip of the road to spin at some frantic speed. We crashed back to earth, and the jolt destroyed the roof rack, and our bakelite suitcases bounced and rolled alongside us, and burst, scattering clothing across the desert. Somehow, I managed to prevent the car from careering off into the desert to join our clothing, and we came to a stop, askew but still on the road, and we sat for a while to get over our shock.

We got out of the car and walked around it. Apart from the roof rack, it looked undamaged. Mungo got back into the car, started the engine and gingerly let in the clutch. The car moved forward. We collected our clothes, threw them in the back of the car, climbed in and went on our way. I was relegated to the back seat, where I could ponder my shortcomings.

The car no longer seemed to go as fast as it could before we went into the sky, and that kept us on edge for a while. However, we were not lying in the desert next to the burnt-out frame of an upturned car, and our good fortune began to sink in.

There were miles to go before we slept, and the valley floor had another surprise in store for us. A small mud-brick hut came into view, and as we drew nearer, we saw that there was a chain across the road, slung between two small posts. We came to a halt, and a man came out of the hut. He was dressed in a dark blue uniform, with a stripe down his trousers and metal buttons on his jacket. He put on a cap. He came to the car and talked to us. We talked to him. But there was no common language. We pointed, indicating we wanted to continue. He mimed sleeping, and we understood that we were meant to wait here until the next morning.

In the curious way of the Indian subcontinent, other people appeared where there was no one a moment before. Where had they come from? The hut was too small. Now we were surrounded by people dressed as if they had just come off the set of a Shaftesbury Avenue production of *The Desert Song*, except, that is, for, the dust, the penetrating gaze of desert-dwellers, and the fact that the .303 rifles they had slung over their shoulders were real. One of the cast reached in the driver's window, and pulled Mungo's left arm out of the car. Would an enormous knife come down, severing the hand from the rest of Mungo? No, the desert song man was inspecting Mungo's watch. Now there was a loud discussion between the man in uniform and the eight tribesmen. Again they indicated that we should sleep there, and again we indicated that we wanted to go on.

There was a pause in which nothing happened. Then the man in the uniform wandered away and stood looking out across the valley floor. We looked around. The rest of them were doing the same. After all these years, I can find no other explanation: they were looking away so that they could say that they had not seen us leave. There were padlocks attaching the chain to the posts, so we drove into the desert and around the post on the left, and back on to the road. We drove on. I looked out the back window and the tribesmen and the man in uniform were still studiously not looking in our direction.

The light went from the sky, the car had no real speed, and we drove through darkness for the last hour (without drifting off the road) before reaching our destination. We found a place to stay, that is, a place with some shelter, where we could spread out our sleeping bags. I lay in the dark and had the horrors for a while, thinking of what might have happened. But it hadn't, and I was twenty-three, and had just proved that we were immortal. I went to sleep.

The next morning, we found the village tea house, and fairly soon after we sat down, a man joined us. He spoke excellent English, and announced that he was the local tax collector. We told him about flying the car, and he said he could take us to someone in the village who could jack the car up and have a look at it.

'My friend has an oxyacetylene welding kit,' he said.

It sounded unlikely but turned out to be true. The friend welded what looked like a crack in the chassis.

We also told the tax collector about the man in uniform, the tribesmen and the chain across the road, and he said that the tribesmen were paid to stop people travelling on the road at night. There were bandits who came across the border from Afghanistan and preyed upon people travelling at night.

'Prey upon?' David asked.

'My word yes,' the tax collector said. 'They murder them.'

Talking of murder

In London in 1964, I worked for several months for a small company that hired out self-drive cars and provided a limousine with a chauffeur for those very special occasions. The limo was an Austin Princess all black and shiny and old-fashioned-looking. The chauffeur was me. I did two kinds of job. I would pick up clients from Heathrow airport and drive them to their destination, usually a posh hotel in the West End, and on Saturdays I would do the weddings.

The weddings could be dispiriting affairs. I would pick up the bride from some down-at-heel pub, drive her to a nearby church, hang about talking to the photographer, then drive the couple to another pub for a down-at-heel reception. Some of the couples were so awkward with each other that I suspected they were meeting face to face for the first time.

I came into work one day and the boss told me to take one of the self-drive hire cars, pick up a client and drive to Heathrow to pick up a second client arriving from the USA. I was to remain at the disposal of the two clients for the rest of the day.

'Shouldn't I take the limo?'

'No. The client said she wanted something ordinary.'

I drove to a large house in Primrose Hill, a wealthy part of London. There I picked up a woman of about fifty. She was dressed in ordinary clothes, as if she had put down whatever she was doing about the house and walked straight out the front door the moment I knocked. Her manner, however, was anything but relaxed. She was clutching a handbag, and she continued clutching it when she got into the car. Once in the car, she looked into the handbag twice, in rapid succession. She looked tired.

We drove to Heathrow, where we picked up a man at about ten a.m. The man had an American accent. He got into the car and he and the woman greeted each other perfunctorily. The woman then instructed me to drive to the Kennington Registry.

On the way back into London, the couple did not talk. We arrived at the Kennington Registry for Births, Deaths and Marriages. I parked outside the registry and got out to open the door but the couple did not move. After a minute or two, they got out. Both looked very tense. They climbed the steps slowly and went into the building. I hung about smoking, which is what chauffeurs did.

Some half an hour later, the couple emerged, and they were transformed. Both were smiling broadly. Their arms were linked. They kept looking at each other and laughing delightedly. They got back into the car.

The woman dropped her handbag carelessly on the seat beside her. 'My friend has a flight back to the USA at six p.m. so could you take us back to the airport? He has not been to London before so can you go through Trafalgar Square and past Buckingham Palace?'

This I did. The man and the woman chatted, but about nothing to indicate what they had registered at the registry. A marriage? I think not. They knew each other well, it seemed, but did not relate to each other like lovers. A birth? The couple were not in their first blush of youth. A death?

The drive from the registry to Heathrow was incident-free. We dropped the man off at the airport, about six hours after we had picked him up, and I drove the woman back to Holland Park. She was chatty, all of it inconsequential and none of it about the purpose of the day. I dropped her off and drove back to the office. There I hung up my chauffeur's cap, which the woman had asked me not to wear, and headed off to the pub, where the firm's two mechanics and I usually had a drink at the end of the day. It was, they reminded me, my round.

During that and the next round, I thought about my day. It did not feel right. Why would the man fly back and forth across the Atlantic on the same day? Weird. Why the fear, and then relief when the business in the registry was completed? What was that business, and did money change hands? Was there a corpse propped up on a sofa back at the Primrose Hill house?

And what about those woeful weddings? Had the priest and my boss cornered some kind of market in human trafficking? Were the 'brides' being unknowingly drawn into the slave trade? Was the car hire a front? Was I part of that front!

What could I do? Go to the police? I had not actually seen anything untoward. I calmed down. I had been letting my imagination run wild. Ridiculous. Even so, I resigned the next day.

Risking life and limb in London

In London in the 1960s, work was plentiful. You could walk out of one job in the morning and into another in the afternoon – an exaggeration, no doubt, but that's what it felt like.

I spent three weeks working with a mob of out-of-work actors hanging 'a fabulous cascade of Venetian glass' from the ceiling of London's Olympia Exhibition Hall. We clambered around on towers of scaffolding, metres above a concrete floor, without a sniff of a safety harness, and it is a miracle none of us was killed.

I had heard about the job on the grapevine and turned up at the exhibition hall on the off chance. As I approached the worksite, I saw two towers of scaffolding with people moving about on them. I do not like heights and I turned away. It was not for me. But at that moment, I heard a woman's voice calling out my name. I turned and looked up. The woman – we had acted together in a show a few months earlier – was hailing me from the topmost level of one of the towers of scaffolding. A ludicrous machismo took hold of me. I reported to the site foreman and was climbing the tower of scaffolding five minutes later.

I was sharing a flat at the time with Clive James and Bruce Beresford. That evening, all three of us were in, and I told them about the job. They were impressed.

'No reactions?' Clive asked. 'Like suddenly freezing and having to be strapped into a stretcher and lowered whimpering to the ground?'

'Nothing like that,' I said. 'It took me about half an hour to get used to the height. After that, everything was fine.'

I was feeling dead-tired and so made my excuses and headed off to bed. I read for a while and then switched off the light and within seconds was shivering and shaking. This was interspersed by great juddering, involuntary spasms. Gradually, the spasms and then the shivering subsided and when they had stopped altogether, I saw that I had kicked the bedclothes off and that they were strewn across the floor. I lay for a while wondering whether I had shouted out, but neither Bruce nor Clive came to my bedroom door, so I probably had not. I remade my bed and got into it. My body was racked by one final isolated spasm, and I fell into an exhausted sleep.

The job may have been life-threatening but it was relatively easy. A great square made up of steel girders had been hoisted up and secured against the ceiling of the exhibition hall. Steel cables had been welded into place across the square to form a grid, and where the cables intersected we attached wires from which dangled pieces of coloured glass. The pieces of glass were hung on different lengths of wire, and gradually the fabulous cascade took shape.

The pieces of glass had been manufactured in a factory on one of the Venetian islands, and delivered to London in massive wooden boxes, accompanied by a Venetian, who supervised us and ensured that we were following the design. One small problem was that he had no English, but luckily one of the women in the team spoke some Italian and acted as an interpreter.

The pieces of glass were the size of two milk bottles and heavy. As the chandelier grew, some of us began wondering whether the steel grid would carry the full weight of the chandelier when it was finished. During the course of the exhibition, hundreds – no, thousands – of people would be wandering about, many of them passing directly under the chandelier and some no doubt stopping to chat or to look at the exhibition program and decide where they might go next. Unwitting parents would summon little children to stand with them directly under several tons of Venetian glass that had been strung above them by a group of unemployed actors.

The anxiety of some of us grew and we finally sought the help of our interpreter and asked the Venetian whether he felt the chandelier would hold or whether it would come crashing down. The Venetian replied, and we crowded around the interpreter and asked her what he had said.

'He said,' she said, 'that the longer it stays up, the longer it will stay up.'

A saner or less venal person might well have left the country immediately, phoning the police anonymously just before catching the ferry from Dover. But I stayed until the job was finished, and turned up after the exhibition was over to go aloft again and help dismantle the fabulous contraption. The money was good. We were paid in cash. There was no mention of Her Majesty's Department of Inland Revenue and Customs (that is, the UK tax office).

PS: Clive we have already touched upon. Bruce has become a successful and much admired film director. His films are too many to list but his finest in my opinion are *Mister Johnson* and *The Black Robe*. His best known are probably *Driving Miss Daisy* and *Tender Mercies*.

Telling the world's longest joke in Covent Garden

Early on in my time in London, I acquired a sound system consisting of a microphone, amplifier and two speakers. I had the mad idea of trying my hand at stand-up comedy. Do not ask me why, because I cannot think of anything more stressful. It was just another example of the retreat-approach conflict I had with performance for over a decade. I put the system aside but could not bring myself to throw it away, so it travelled with me from one bedsitter to the next, until it came into its own in early 1968.

I had been involved in a minor way with the London *OZ* magazine, 'the organ of the swinging sixties'. I knew Richard Neville, the editor, and Jim Anderson, one of the co-editors, and I had written an article for the magazine's first edition. Some of this may go to explain why I listened, instead of heading for the nearest exit, when Andrew Fisher, another *OZ* luminary, asked me to participate in an *OZ* benefit he was organising. The event would take place in Middle Earth, a basement club in Covent Garden, and would involve several rock bands, a couple of DJs, and me.

Andrew had come up with the idea that I tell the world's longest joke. He had heard me tell jokes in pubs and parties, and he liked an old-fashioned circular shaggy-dog joke called 'The deep apple Syrian pie joke'. In this joke, each time the story seems to be coming to an end, it somehow slips a cog and begins all over again.

OZ survived and occasionally flourished because of Andrew. In amongst the people wearing Afghan coats and strings of multicoloured beads, he was the one who could manage and administer. Now he told me he would organise a small stage in a corner of Middle Earth well away from the main stages where the rock groups would be playing.

He would arrange several rows of seating in front of my stage, so that people could sit and listen. And did I still have that microphone, amplifier, and speakers because, if I did, it saved him the trouble of organising that too?

When the day came, I thought of not turning up but, after a drink in a nearby pub, I lugged my sound system down the steps into Middle Earth, found my corner perfectly set up, set my own system up, tested it and found it to be satisfactorily loud. I donned my truly awful orange and yellow paisley shirt, took up my position, and waited until the first rock group had completed a very long set.

It was now about ten p.m. and one of the DJs announced that I would be starting the world's longest joke. A crowd gathered in front of me and I began. The story itself has some moments and my audience laughed, and when I finished the first cycle and started repeating the story, people laughed and clapped. A new rock group began their set, and people wandered away.

The evening wore on. Ten became eleven. The DJs announced that I was still telling the joke. People came, listened for a while and left. Some came back to check that I was still going. Eleven drifted into midnight. I sat down but went on telling the story. I paused for a drink of water and went on. Midnight became one a.m. I felt myself growing tired. I knew enough to have begun quietly, letting the sound system do the amplifying, but my voice began to go hoarse anyway. As we approached two a.m., I cheated. When an up-and-coming group took the stage, and all eyes were on them, I stopped altogether and rested for fifteen minutes. I took up the joke where I had left off and felt dizzy for a moment. I realised that the heavy fug was getting to me. But the fug also relaxed me and I passed though a period of mild euphoria and started chuckling at my own joke. At some stage, the DJ who had announced me came over and asked me how I was going. I said I was all right.

The DJ clearly decided that I was not all right. He went back to the main stage and announced that the world's longest joke was coming to an end. He had not warned me, and people turned to see me scrambling back on stage. There was laughter as the crowd pushed across the floor space and into my corner. I took up the joke again and told a whole cycle. I sidestepped the stratagem that set the whole cycle going again, and told the punchline, which was

'Oh, that's all right, then. I'll have peaches and cream.'

I do not think it would have mattered what I said. People were there for the event of the punchline, not the punchline itself, and so they laughed and clapped and cheered. It was somewhere between two and three a.m. (or between one and two, I didn't really know…). The DJ called the audience back to the main stage, introduced the next group, and the evening thundered on.

Andrew and I packed up and pushed through the crowd to the exit. I got some smiles and slaps on the back as I went. We came out into early morning Covent Garden. Andrew fetched his car, and I put the speakers and amplifier in the boot. We went back inside for no more than ten minutes, and when we got back, the boot door had been forced (by an opera-goer, I assumed) and my sound equipment was gone.

I was exhausted and hallucinating. I wanted to go home. The equipment was out of date. I was not going to use it again. And the theft had a kind of symbolism to it. Inside were lots of people caught up in the so-called swinging sixties. Many believed that the world had changed forever. After all, it was only a few months since the so-called summer of love. But outside it was London, not California, and an arbitrary and sometimes unpleasant world prevailed.

Just a little more about *OZ*. The magazine pushed the boundaries of taste with every edition, challenging the constraints of both law and convention, until the editors were charged with obscenity and had to face trial at the Old Bailey. Found guilty on one of the charges, they spent three days in prison, where they had their hair forcibly cut. Oddly, this seemed to excite the press and the protesters more than issues of human rights and the freedom of the press.

OZ also pushed the boundaries of typography, under the inspired guidance of the artist Martin Sharp. In the later editions, each page was a work of art, a magnificent display of colourful patterns of typescript against sometimes matching, sometimes clashing backgrounds. Martin created a body or work made up of paintings, posters, collages, and a series of portraits of significant figures of the 1960s, including a stunning depiction of Jimi Hendrix performing in concert. Search it out, and marvel.

Falling in love

This should be an extra special highlight in which I tell the story of Marianne's and my falling in love. The trouble is that, over the centuries, a not inconsiderable number of writers, good, bad and indifferent, have told the same story. How then do I tell Marianne's and my version without writing in clichés?

It was 1966. I was in London, and out of work. I had noticed a slightly dilapidated Regency house near my bedsitter in Kensington. It had a small sign on the front gate announcing that it was the home of the Linguists' Club School of English. I went in, and asked at the office to see the person in charge. After a brief wait, a tall, weary-looking man came out of an inner office and offered a limp hand in greeting. I guessed that the powers that-be-in that inner office had told him to get rid of me as soon as possible.

I had never taught English as a foreign language, but I told him I had. He edged me towards the door and I told him I was very good at teaching English as a foreign language. He continued his edging but I held my ground. I had, I told him, lots of experience of teaching English as a foreign language in both Greece and Italy.

He slowed, stopped, thought, and then said, 'We have an intermediate course that meets on three evenings a week.'

His mood had changed, and I suspected that he was the current teacher of said evening class.

'I can do that,' I said. 'When do you want me to start?'

My first few evenings as an expert teacher of English as a foreign language were untidy but I must have done something right because, after six weeks of doing the night shift, I was promoted to daytime classes and given five mornings a week.

The teaching was fun. There were rarely more than twelve in a class so a lot of the teaching and learning was done through amiable (if sometimes tortured) conversation.

The classes were made up of people from a variety of European countries, and a sprinkling of people from elsewhere (Iran and Turkey, mainly).

The teachers made up a rum bunch. The students dressed well, some of the men in in suits, but the teachers dressed in a style best called English scruffy. As it turned out, all of us had fled other professions. David Brown had abandoned a university career. He was a gifted teacher, and a depressive. Sometimes he would arrive in the morning, his face creased as if in physical pain. Gradually, the creases would disappear and, particularly in the second class in the morning and the first in the afternoon, he would become an inspired and hilarious teacher. The second session in the afternoon would see the creases return. John Basing had graduated from Oxford in 1954 and begun writing a novel, which he was still cheerfully working on when I last saw him in 2015. Yes, 2015. Jimmy James had been on the beaches of Dunkirk, and then in the Benghazi handicap. We discovered after his death that he had a doctorate in divinity. Geraldine had abandoned a number of jobs that might have made use of her degree in mathematics. O'Brien (I never learnt his first name) was on retreat from chemical engineering, and I, as you know, had fled journalism.

When I felt I was an established member of the teaching staff, I approached the principal and suggested that I teach a course in the afternoons on T.S. Eliot's *The Wasteland*. By having something like that in the program, I said, we would steal a march on our competitors. My own motives were, of course, to earn more money.

The course was duly advertised and it attracted eight people. One of them was Marianne.

The course, like virtually everything else about this eccentric institution, was good fun. We set about unravelling Eliot's language and going in pursuit of his allusions and references. (Eliot makes this enterprise possible by attaching to the poem a number of explanatory notes.)

I asked Marianne out and, sitting opposite her in a Chelsea restaurant, I became entranced by this gently spoken, serious-minded, quietly amused Frenchwoman. During the evening, Marianne explained that she had not come to London to brush up her English, but rather to gain some respite from her oppressive mother. But the pressures to return to Paris – the vituperative letters, the angry phone calls – were becoming increasingly difficult to ignore. At the end of the evening, we lingered in the shadows a little back from the front door of the house she was lodged in. We held each other tight and, like sensible (idiot) adults, we acknowledged that this moment had come too terribly late in her stay in London.

Three days later, she was gone.

I taught listlessly for a few days, until a student twice my age from Iran told me, sympathetically, to get my act together. Coming from his mouth in his accent, the idiom sounded wonderful. I burst into laughter, and the skies cleared.

I thought of Marianne often, but I did not write. I am not sure why. Perhaps I could not bear the sweet sorrow of another parting.

I was still teaching at the Linguists' Club School of English ten months later, and the principal caught up with me in the hallway.

She said she had a letter from Marianne, and went on, 'She asks me if Mr Newman is still teaching here. I am assuming you are happy for me to reply saying "Yes".'

The principal looked at me. I stood for a moment. No matter how much fun the Linguists' Club School of English might have been, I had been drifting.

'Yes, please,' I said. 'Yes. Write to her saying yes. Yes,' I said once more, and we both laughed with delight.

Making arrangements in Versailles

My father was a thinker, a theologian and social theorist, and author of a book called *Freedom and control*, in which he sought to update the ideas of a group of London lawyers, writers, artists and clerics from the 1850s who had called themselves the Christian Socialists.

Dad talked slowly, with a broad Australian accent, was observant, and indulged in a gentle kind of humour that people could miss if they did not notice the wry smile. His taste in food was old-fashioned Aussie, with boiled carrots in white sauce at or very near the top of the list. I know you might think this last piece of information gratuitous, but I assure you that it is not.

My marriage was an arranged one. As already told, Marianne and I had met in London in 1966, and by 1968 were in what was turning out to be a serious relationship. As far as we were concerned, we were living together but as far as France was concerned we were not. I was teaching English as a foreign language in the Linguists' Club School of English in the mornings and making a film with Bruce Beresford and Andrew Fisher (for whom I had told the world's longest joke) in the afternoons. Marianne had fallen in love with me and I had fallen in love with her. How do we explain these things? Did she like the shape of my backside as I turned to write on the blackboard? She won't tell.

All this to say that it seemed perfectly normal for me to introduce Marianne to my parents when they came for a three-week visit to London in early 1968. This was duly done in a restaurant in South Kensington, and my parents were delighted.

My mother and father had scheduled a week in Paris after they had surfeited themselves on theatre in London. Marianne's family was Parisian, and again it seemed normal to arrange a meeting with her parents and mine. The first meeting took place in Marianne's parents' apartment in the seventh arrondissement, and the formality with which this was done should have alerted Marianne and me to the dangers ahead, but, perhaps because of the novelty of the situation, it did not.

Marianne's mother Mathilde greeted us at the door of the apartment and took us to the salon. There we sat, and I watched in admiration as my mother reactivated the French she had learnt at the University of Melbourne circa 1919. Dad, who had no language other than English, smiled awkwardly.

A few minutes later, Marianne's father Achille arrived. He was a tall and elegant former naval officer – commandant, capitaine de corvette, Legion d'Honneur – and he strode into the salon, went straight to my mother, bent from the waist, and lifted and kissed the back of her hand. My mother's face was a mixture of shock and delight. Achille then turned to my father, who grabbed both arms of his chair and began to rise. I could see the near panic in his face. What was he meant to do? Would this Frenchman try to kiss him? French men did kiss each other, didn't they? Dad pulled himself up to full height, which meant that his eyes were about where Achille would wear his medals. He braced himself but to his enormous relief Marianne's father made no attempt to embrace him, and they simply shook hands.

From the apartment, we went to Lasserre. Again, Marianne and I should have seen the warning signs but we did not. La Tour d'Argent is the Paris restaurant where international celebrities go. Lasserre is the Paris restaurant where Parisians go. Both cost a fortune.

Marianne's father organised the seating and placed me next to my father to give him moral support. My mother was placed on Achille's right and was in seventh heaven. We were handed menus the size of bed sheets. I admit that is an exaggeration but they were big, and we settled down to read them.

Dad looked at the menu with oysters, truffles, caviar, snails and a multitude of other culinary joys on offer, and said quietly to me, 'Do you reckon they have a clear chicken soup here?'

As was often the case with Dad, I couldn't be sure whether he was being serious or joking.

Back at our hotel, I called in on my parents' room to say goodnight. Mum was still excited about the evening, but her mood changed as I was about to leave. I was confirming arrangements for the next day: Marianne would be picking us up at the hotel at ten thirty and taking us, together with her mother, to visit the Palace of Versailles.

My mum, who was nobody's mug, looked at me and said, 'Whatever you do tomorrow, boy, do not leave us alone with that woman.'

We got to Versailles late the next morning, and walked through the gates and into the enormous cobbled forecourt to the palace. Marianne and I hung back to talk and did not register that my parents and Marianne's mother had disappeared into the passageway in the far right-hand corner of the forecourt that leads through to the gardens on the other side of the palace.

Time passed and suddenly we saw my mum hurrying back. She was having trouble controlling her laughter.

'Boy,' she said, 'you are married!'

'What do you mean?'

'I told you not to leave us alone. The moment you were out of earshot, Mathilde asked me to ask your dad whether he minded you marrying a Catholic.'

'What did dad say?'

'He said to me, "They haven't talked of marriage, have they?" I said, "That's not the question." Your dad said, "What do I say?" And I said, "Oh no, you don't. She's asking you. I'm just the interpreter."'

'So?' I asked.

'So your father says, "Well, I don't mind Michael marrying a Catholic, do I?" And I translate that to Marianne's mother, and she says, "Ask your husband if Tuesday, 17 September will be all right."'

A brush with revolution in Paris

In February 1968, a columnist in a French newspaper announced that the country was doing well but nothing of interest was happening. The president was bored and the people were bored, the columnist said. And yet, in early May, a little over two months later, there were riots in Paris, barricades in the streets, overturned cars, massive demonstrations in all the major cities, and pitched battles with the police.

Borders were closed. Some ten million workers, including car workers, staff and journalists from the national television channels, teachers, road cleaners, and professional footballers (yes!) were on strike. How did all this start? On the evening of 3 May 1968, students gathered at the Sorbonne in the quartier latin in Paris to protest about overcrowding in universities in general, and about the authorities' heavy-handed response to any form of protest in particular. The numbers of students grew and the university authorities called the police. Arrests were made, and a battle ensued which went through the night. Students and police were injured. Over the next week, the battles and demonstrations escalated. The country ground to a halt, and many believed that a full-scale revolution was under way.

Their fears were understandable. There were some ten or more days in that troubled May when the country was in paralysis, the government very shaky, and anything could have happened. Meetings were being held by alliances of politicians and prominent figures with a view to filling the gap if the government fell. Amidst the confusion, President de Gaulle flew out of the country to Germany to reassure himself that the French troops stationed there would remain loyal to him, leaving the country without a head of government in place for twelve hours!

On or about 15 May, Marianne's father Achille rang me from Paris.

The automated international exchange was still working. Marianne was back in Paris at the time, and she acted as interpreter. Marianne and I were scheduled to marry in September, but it was important, Achille said, that we bring the wedding forward. He did not spell it out, but I got the impression that he thought he was going to lose everything. His (patriarchal) response to this was to ensure that his daughter was married as soon as possible to a husband who would be able to look after her if he (Achille) were taken away in a tumbril. Until then, I had felt that Achille was anything but keen for his daughter to marry an Australian living a cheap bedsitter existence in London, but his attitude had changed, and I have all those rioters to thank for that.

'You have to come to France and begin the paperwork for your marriage,' Achille said.

I had not thought about paperwork until then, but of course we are talking about French bureaucracy, and of course there would be paperwork, and it would be more than normal because I was a foreigner.

I hung up and headed down the hill from my small rented London flat to Kensington High Street and into the local Thomas Cook's office. I went to the counter. It was mid-morning.

'Can I help you, sir?'

'I hope so. I want to get to Paris urgently. Today if possible.'

The man looked startled. The papers and television were full of stories every day about France. Scenes of police equipped with helmets, shields and batons standing across streets in a mass and ready to charge, people atop the barricades, people ripping up and throwing cobblestones, clouds of tear gas…scenes of events halfway between demonstration and urban combat.

'I'm not sure we can do that, sir. The French borders are closed.'

'Can you just check?'

The man picked up the phone and dialled. He was put on hold, and we waited. Then someone came on at the other end of the line. The Thomas Cook's man spoke quickly, and was put on hold again, and we waited. Someone came on again.

'Could you hold just a moment?' the Thomas Cook's man said into the phone, and then looked up at me, smiling, proudly. 'There is only one flight by any airline into France today,' he said. 'The flight is at three thirty p.m. and the airline is British European Airways.' He could not have sounded more patriotic if 'Rule Britannia' had been playing in the background. We fixed up the ticket for the flight from Heathrow and I headed for the airport.

The plane was a Trident. It was full of people. They could not all be going to get the paperwork ready to marry a French person, so why did they want to get into a country in a state of upheaval? Everyone kept to her or himself. None of this chatty 'And why are you going to Paris?' Just a sea of closed faces.

We landed at a military base, and the Trident came to a halt at the end of the runway. There was a man with a set of stairs on wheels but nothing and no one else. The business part of the airport, the hangars, office blocks and so on, were barely visible at the other end of a long runway built, I assumed, to accommodate those huge transport aircraft. We left the plane and stood about on the tarmac.

The captain descended the stairs, and said in a plummy accent, 'I wonder whether some of the gentlemen could help unload the luggage.'

Some of us helped and now we were standing about on the tarmac along with a pile of luggage. Then, in the fading light, we could see two coaches driving towards us along the runway. They arrived, some of us gentlemen helped load the luggage, and we got in and set off for Paris. The coaches dropped us in the Champs Élysées, we took our bags, and one by one we slipped away into the night. There had been no passport checks.

Marianne and I went to the town hall in the seventh arrondissement the next morning to begin the paperwork. The place was open and the people we spoke to were happy to respond. This set me thinking. If the town halls across the country were open, then the country was functioning at an administrative level and the anarchy that Achillle feared was not happening. I did see a huge demonstration later that day, swinging its merry way down the rue de Rivoli. And Marianne and I went into the Sorbonne after midnight, where we listened to workers in their blue overalls addressing a mob of students in one of the courtyards. We wandered through the buildings, coming upon a lecture theatre full of people engaged in noisy debate and another housing a concert of second-rate jazz. The mood was edgy and elated, but nothing suggested the arrival of a new post-enlightenment, post-capitalist, post-socialist, post-postmodern world.

Marianne was studying at the time at the British Institute, whose premises were nearby. She had heard that institute students had occupied the premises in sympathy with what was happening at the Sorbonne. We went to see. The entrance was guarded by an unpleasant-looking young man.

'We want to go in,' Marianne said in French. The unpleasant young man just looked at her.

'We want to go in,' I said in English.

'You can't.'

'Why not?'

'We have occupied the building.'

'Who's we?'

'The students.'

'But I am a student here,' Marianne said, 'so let us in.'

'No.'

At that moment, another equally unpleasant young man appeared in the corridor and approached us. 'What's the matter?' he said in English to the gatekeeper.

'Nothing,' the gatekeeper said. 'Just a couple of bourgeois.'

The pigs had already taken control of the farm. Boxer, the amiable, ever accommodating, hard-working draught horse, was long gone to the knacker's yard. We wandered away. I have been a member of the appropriate trade union throughout my working life, and I have never voted for any party other than the British Labour Party or the Australian Labor Party. There I was in Paris at what could have been a turning point in history. It would be easy, by virtue of a meaningful silence to give the impression that I was there in the streets and occasionally racing forward from the crowd to pick up a tear gas canister and hurl it back at the line of police. But I did no such thing. I was not there to man the barricades. I was there to get the paperwork done so that I could marry a Parisian girl of good family.

'Just a couple of bourgeois,' the gatekeeper had said.

PS: And how did it all end? The Communist Party, a real force in French politics at the time, was ostensibly a revolutionary party, but they opted to behave like a union instead and go for a wage increase of ten per cent across the board. Activist workers, steeped in Marx, had never wholeheartedly fallen in with the students. Student slogans such as 'Be realistic, demand the impossible' and 'It is forbidden to forbid' may have reflected a joyful rebelliousness but they did not inspire confidence in seasoned political heavyweights. On 29 May, the Confédération Générale du Travail, a peak left-wing union body, held a huge demonstration and effectively wrested the control of the protests from the hands of the students. On 30 May, President De Gaulle dissolved the Assemblie Nationale and announced elections in June. The election campaign gathered speed. Summer was coming, and the holidays beckoned.

Signing the marriage contract

When I got to France to sort out the paperwork for our marriage, Marianne told me that I had to sign a marriage contract. 'What's that?' I asked, and she said that in our case the contract would say that my wealth would remain mine, and that Marianne's wealth, present and inherited, would remain hers. I had no wealth to squabble about, and it came as a shock that anyone might think I had designs on whatever money Marianne might have.

'I have no wealth to squabble about,' I said to Marianne, 'and it comes as a shock that people might think that I had designs on anything you had.'

'I know, I know,' she said, 'but my mother thought it the wise thing to do…'

'Did she?'

'Don't do it for her. Do it for me.'

What could I say? And so, late the next afternoon, with France still tottering on the brink of revolution, I found myself sitting in a lawyer's office on the first floor of a building in the Rue de Rivoli, listening to one of two men in very serious dark grey suits explain the minutiae of what I was about to sign. I tried to understand for a while but was distracted by a large red banner (the communists), then a large black banner (the anarchists), bouncing past the avocat's first- floor windows.

I shifted my seat a little so that I could look along the street. It had been empty when we arrived but was now packed with demonstrators waving banners, singing and shouting and chanting, and coalescing into a single massive crowd.

The avocat kept on reading. I tugged at Marianne's sleeve, and spoke over the increasing row from outside. 'Can you tell him that the world is falling apart right under his window.'

Marianne hesitated, and then tried to interrupt the avocat's flow. He appeared to ignore her, but then, without taking his eyes off the text, he raised his right hand, let the fingers hang limp, and, leading with his little finger, waved the whole hand in the direction of the demonstrators, as if shooing away an annoying fly.

Sri Lankans can communicate whole paragraphs by gesturing with their heads and hands. I would bet that they are the best in the world at this. But the French are not far behind. That avocat's gesture was redolent with meaning. 'Those little people in the street outside think they are changing the world, but they are not. Long after they have gone, the bourgeois class, of which I am proud to be a member, will still be in control. Now, monsieur, I have a job to do and that is to read the whole of this contract to you, get you to say that you understand it, and then get you to sign it. For the moment nothing else matters.'

When we left the avocat's office and went into the street, apart from more litter than usual, there was little evidence that tens of thousands of people had just marched merrily by.

Marianne and I moved house recently and I came across a yellowing copy of our marriage contract. As far as I know, it has not been referred to once in all the fifty-plus years that Marianne and I have been together.

Divine anger in Paris

On 8 July 1968, Marianne and I were married in the town hall of the seventh arrondissement by a mayor splendidly decked out in some kind of formal attire with a tricolor stretching across his expansive front. He spoke at some length but my French was not up to it. And on 9 July 1968, we were wed all over again, in a religious service at Saint Pierre du Gros Caillou (literally, Saint Peter of the Big Pebble) by a priest decked out in priestly robes. Again, my French was not up to it.

When Marianne had told the priest some weeks earlier that she was going to marry an Australian, he had said that Australian men beat their wives. Marianne tells me the priest was a great scholar with a fine sense of humour, and that may have been true, but I don't think he liked me (or perhaps he didn't like the idea of me). The priest had been Marianne's spiritual director, and I suspect he saw me as a stranger, an uncouth Caliban let loose in the streets of Paris, stealing his beautiful young maiden away.

During the ceremony, the priest turned to Marianne and addressed her by her first name. Then he turned to me and addressed me, using the formal term 'Monsieur'. My brother Sandy, who was studying in France at the time, told me after the ceremony that the difference in the form of address was marked. And I had felt the disapproval. Marianne and I were seated on two chairs in the central aisle of the nave. The priest was standing two steps up on the raised level of the chancel, and I had to tilt my head back (a bit like Rowlf in the Muppets) to look at him. The priest glowered down at me and I had the impression that he was saying that he and his Jesuit mates knew where I lived.

A few years ago, I came across of an essay by William Hazlitt called 'The pleasure of hating'. Hazlitt wrote it in 1826, and in it he gave a wonderful description of a fire and brimstone preacher of the day called Mr Irving, who used 'big words and monstrous denunciations', and was 'like a huge Titan, looking as grim and swarthy as if he had to forge tortures for all the damned'.

I cannot help thinking that the priest at our wedding was driven by the same kind of anger.

Servant and master in Brittany

My father-in-law, Achille, graduated in 1918 from the top naval college in France (la Grande École Navale) without a title or wealth or good connections, but with excellent results. He was posted to a ship and soon afterwards married Mathilde, my mother-in-law-to-be. Achille attracted the attention of his ship's commander, who took him under his wing. The commander's wife was an aristocrat and her family owned a chateau in Brittany. Mathilde and Achille were always welcome there and Marianne remembers going to the chateau for holidays throughout her childhood and teenage years.

The commander's family was irredeemably hospitable. They were a shambles at managing money and the estate. Each summer would end with the family at the chateau owing an enormous amount of money to the village butcher. Three of the brothers owned a ketch in which they transported Breton produce to Morocco, but somehow they never made much money. A number of the family had never worked. Children from the next generation did various things. Some of them failed completely, one committing suicide after a collapsed property deal, and others succeeded, one of them making millions selling T-shirts. One married a millionaire who had a private plane and a full-time pilot. The successful ones supported the family and contributed in a haphazard way to the chateau's upkeep.

Marianne treasured her connection with this family. One of the daughters of the clan had been Marianne's best friend. She had died two years before Marianne and I met. Marianne wanted me to see the place so associated with her childhood and with her friend, and we headed to Brittany after our wedding and spent three days of our honeymoon at the chateau.

The chateau, a bit like the family, was run-down. It dated from the fifteenth century and was made of blue-grey stone and with three towers on the corners topped with conical slate roofs. One of the towers was under repair, with most of the slates removed and newish timber visible in the conical framework. I suspected it had been like that for several months.

The chateau was brooding and dark inside, in keeping with the rainy Breton weather. There were dark tapestries hanging on the walls, and paintings badly in need of cleaning. In the oldest part of the chateau, there was a spiral staircase of greenish stone that rose into the gloom. But if you needed light, there was an eighteenth century wing tacked on to one side of the chateau, with tall windows and doors looking out onto a dishevelled parkland.

At the time of our visit, there were three surviving brothers of the older generation of the clan. Two – Erwann and Loic – lived at the chateau. The other – Mael – lived at another even more run down chateau forty kilometres away. I liked Erwann and Loic immediately. Loic was delighted when he learnt I could play table tennis, and we played for hours on end in a huge attic space above one of the chateau's outbuildings. Erwann showed me around the chateau, including a door to a hidden passageway, and a letter from George Washington to the then head of the Breton clan thanking him for his support in America's struggle against the British.

On our first evening at the chateau, we dined abstemiously on a boiled egg each and some cheese and salad. At bedtime, Erwann told us to get up whenever we liked in the morning, and go to the chateau's kitchen. There would be bread, butter and jam out on the table and everything necessary to make coffee.

Marianne and I woke about eight, and I got up to investigate. The kitchen was a huge space, with a long black table in the centre. As I entered, I saw an elderly woman, dressed in black except for the decorative white Breton apron, seated near one end of the table. Erwann was over by a massive iron cooking range, heating some milk. He introduced me to the woman – Efflama Pichon – and explained that Efflama lived in one of the farms on the estate, and had been a servant to the family since the age of sixteen. Erwann looked at Efflama with evident love in his gaze as he spoke. Efflama was bowed over the table, but looked up at me, smiled and murmured a greeting. Erwann brought the heated milk to Efflama and began pouring it into a bowl in front of her. I watched the master serving the servant.

The perils of drink in the south of France

Marianne and I lived in London for the first fourteen years of our marriage. We spent our summer holidays in the south of France, in a house that my parents-in-law had bought and renovated. The house was in a village called Rocbaron, some fifty or so kilometres from Toulon.

In the summer of 1969, I made a serious error of judgement, and managed to insult two elderly friends of Marianne's parents. Drink had a good bit to do with it, and before we go any further, I accept that being drunk can be an explanation but is not an excuse.

At the time, the house was occupied by my parents-in-law Mathilde and Achille, the elderly friends called Beaunier, the Beauniers' adult son Olivier, Marianne and me. I got on well enough with Olivier but did not like his parents. They were stand-offish, whether because an Australian was simply beyond their ken, or because my small town social class showed through.

But I am beginning to speak in riddles, so let me talk about the paper serviettes. One of Mathilde's close friends had given her a present consisting of hundreds of red paper serviettes with the name of the house – un Petit Coin du Paradis – in gold lettering across one of the corners. My mother-in-law was delighted. I thought the things looked like the kind of serviette you would find in a third-rate hotel trying to look like a second-rate one.

One evening, Marianne and I went out to a restaurant in a village some fifteen kilometres away. Olivier declined my invitation to accompany us and it was clear that he was letting Marianne and me have some time together. Marianne and I ate well, and I drank too much. There were reasons for this. The restaurant specialised in *moules-frites*. The bowl the mussels were served in was enormous, the pile of mussels looked enormous, and because we had to pull each shell apart, it took a long time to eat. The result was that I had the impression that I was eating heartily, but I was not. The *frites* helped a bit, but for the first twenty minutes it was like drinking on an empty stomach. And once I was on my way, it was all too easy to catch the waiter's eye and tap the empty bottle, and another was on the table in an instant.

I was in a merry state when Marianne and I got back to un Petit Coin du Paradis somewhere around one a.m. We let ourselves in by a side door, which opened on to a small corridor, which led to the kitchen. On the kitchen table was a breakfast tray ready to be taken up to the Beauniers. There were two plates to take the croissants, and two bowls to take the coffee. And under each bowl was a red paper serviette, carefully arranged so that the golden words un Petit Coin du Paradis were in full view. It was, I decided, time to act.

The fates are only too happy to assist us when we bring about our own ruination. If I had left the kitchen in search of a pad and pen, then perhaps I might have abandoned or forgotten my plan, and continued upstairs to bed. But there was a pad and pen in the first drawer I opened, and I wrote 'Hotel du Petit Coin du Paradis' at the top of a page and a detailed bill below, with ludicrously large sums against each item. I was writing in French, so put things like '*Boisson* (Drink) 1,450,000 Francs, *Repas* (Meals) 1,900,000 francs'. I slipped the bill into the red serviette under one of the bowls.

My reasoning, which I explained to Marianne, was this: the breakfast tray would be taken up to the Beauniers. They would be sitting up in bed. They would take out the serviettes, open them, and the bill would flutter onto the bedclothes. They would read it and laugh. They would realise that the silly serviettes looked like hotel serviettes. Later in the morning, when they descended into the garden, they would tell Mathilde about my amusing jape, and she too would realise that the silly serviettes looked like hotel serviettes, and would never use them again.

Writing this fifty years later, and sober while doing so, I can see the argument does not convince. But at the time, it seemed foolproof. Marianne's role in all this was minimal. I have asked her over the years why she did not step in and stop me. Perhaps those pesky fates blunted her good sense for a crucial moment. Or more likely, she was not paying attention to anything I was saying or doing.

I slept late and descended into the garden just before lunchtime. I was not feeling well, so was inclined to cut Olivier off when he approached me and said we had to talk. But Olivier was insistent, and led me to a far corner of the garden.

Olivier spoke excellent English, much better than my basic French. 'My parents have received a very perturbing communication.'

I said, 'Oo-ah,' and began giggling because I sounded like Bertie Wooster.

'It is not funny, Mike.'

'Oh.'

'Yes. The communication implies that they are costing your parents-in-law too much money. They say the clear message is that they have overstayed their welcome.'

'They what?'

'They feel insulted and believe whoever wrote the communication is telling them to leave un Petit Coin du Paradis as soon as possible.'

'Look, mate…'

'Why are you calling me mate? I am not your mate.'

'The whole thing was meant to be a joke. Look…I really hate those serviettes, and so Marianne and I –'

'I know nothing about serviettes. Why are you talking to me about serviettes?'

'Tell your parents that I meant no harm. It was a joke directed at my mother-in-law.'

'Why are you talking about Mathilde? I am talking about an insulting note sent to my parents. I know nothing about your mother-in-law. She has nothing to do with this. What are you talking about?'

'God.'

'We shall be having lunch as if everything is normal, and then this afternoon we shall say we have been called away, and all three of us, all three of us, that is my mother, my father and me, we will part.'

'You mean leave?'

'We will depart. We will go. We will leave you here, and we will go away.'

'Jesus.'

'Stop blaspheming!'

'Ah... When I put the note in the serviette...'

'My parents do not want to know who is the author of this note. They are not interesting! Do not tell me what you did or did not do!'

'Give us a break, Olivier. It's obvious who wrote the bloody note. You don't think my father-in-law did, do you? Look, it's been a terrible disaster, but I thought your parents would find it funny.'

'Funny! You must be mad.'

'I feel dreadful.'

'I do not want to know how you feel about anything. I am having enough trouble with my parents' feelings.'

'Olivier, Olivier. Can you please tell your parents none of it was directed at them. It was a joke. A joke. I meant it as a joke. A joke.'

'Well, *mon vieux*, it was a joke that did not work.'

'You can say that again.'

The Beauniers were as good as their word. We all lunched in the garden at the big stone table under the plane tree. Everyone was very polite to everyone else. Monsieur Beaunier made a phone call mid-afternoon, and announced that they would have to cut their stay short. A business matter had come up in Avignon, and from there they would push on to Paris. Their stay had been marvellous, but all good things must come to an end. We all gathered at the large gate at the end of the garden, where the Beauniers' car was parked. Everyone said their farewells as if everything were normal.

Olivier seemed to have calmed down a bit, and he took me a little to one side and said, 'The one good thing out of all this is that no one has told your mother-in-law.'

I nodded. So much for the best-laid schemes o' mice an' men.

For close on a decade, my mother-in-law trotted out those red serviettes whenever she had guests, and people often complimented her on them. Usually, Marianne and I would join the guests at the table, and sometimes, when I flapped my serviette open, I would grimace, and maybe even groan, at the memory it evoked.

'Stop doing that,' Marianne would say, *sotto voce* and in English.

PS: When we first went to Rocbaron in 1969, the village had a population of eighty souls in winter and a hundred and twenty in summer. Fourteen years later, when we made our last visit before leaving Europe for Australia, the village had grown. The summer population had become something more like four hundred. But the village remained compact, and still felt small.

The nearest city was Toulon and to get there you had to drive down a narrow mountain road, on to the costal plain, and through kilometres of industrial estates. Getting to Toulon could take well over an hour. Get caught behind a truck pushing its way out of one of those industrial estates, and the trip could take an hour and a half.

We visited the house at Rocbaron when we were in Europe in 1992. In our absence, the authorities had constructed a four-lane road, which ran down the centre of a neighbouring valley, radically cutting the driving time to Toulon. Rocbaron became a dormitory suburb to Toulon. Small box-like houses proliferated, and the population exploded.

I dwell on these details for a reason. An architect friend visited us at Rocbaron sometime in the early 1970s, and he and I walked up to the end of the valley past a ruined chapel to the remnants of a fort from the days of the Cathards.

He and I stood there admiring the view, and my friend said, 'See those houses.' He pointed to a small line of houses being built just outside the village boundary. 'You can see how the village is spreading. It won't be long before that kind of development stretches unbroken from Calais to Bombay.'

Spirits dashed, we walked down the side of the valley and back to un Petit Coin de Paradis.

1970s

Rock Concerts in London and Saint Tropez

Marianne and I have been at two truly great rock concerts.

The first was in June 1967, and was by the Jimi Hendrix Experience. It took place on a Sunday night in the Saville Theatre on Shaftesbury Avenue in London's West End. Hendrix was acknowledged as one of the most inventive rock guitarists in the world, and the Experience was making its mark as a leading rock band: raw, vital, improvised, savage; a riposte to the lilting melodies of the Beatles, the concocted frenzy of the Who and the posturing of the Rolling Stones.

The theatre was packed and the Experience was everything we had expected. Yes, Hendrix played his guitar with his teeth. And yes again, Hendrix used his guitar to demolish the stand on which Mitch Mitchell was perched with his drum kit. One of the legs of the stand gave way, and drums rolled about on the stage and into the audience, until Mitchell was left on a precarious angle, holding on to single kettledrum and beating it with a single drumstick. And yes again, Hendrix poured lighter fluid over his guitar and set it alight, while Noel Redding continued to punctuate the air (and the smoke) with the relentless rhythm of his bass guitar. And if that were not memorable enough, there was the Experience's performance of 'Hey Joe'.

'Hey Joe' is a dialogue between Joe and a friend. The singer, in this case Hendrix, sings both parts. It is a song about murder and self-destruction. It has something of the call-and-response to be found in the work songs from the south of the USA. The friend asks the questions, and Joe answers. And the song repeats whole lines in a way that is reminiscent of the twelve-bar blues.

Although the story is of vicious, uncompromising vengeance, it is expressed through a subtle melody line, and, on the evening we heard him, when Hendrix started singing, his voice was soft, his tone regretful, as if in anticipation of the horror that was going to unfold. When he reached the end of the second verse, where Joe talks of shooting his lady, Hendrix stepped back from the microphone and played. Hendrix was unique. He could make a single guitar sound like three. He seemed able simultaneously to play a melody line, crashing chords and single, soaring notes coming from nowhere. Hendrix's guitar retold the story and commented upon it, expressing Joe's madness, his truculence and his whining self-justification. This solo was long, and beautiful and disturbing, and then Hendrix was back at the microphone.

The call and response, and the repetitions, were still there, but Hendrix and Mitchell and Reddy were breaking the song down, disturbing the flow with disruptive rhythms and discordant figures. Hendrix was abandoning the form of the previous verses and singing snatches of lines, phrases and single words that voiced the horror and reality of a vengeance killing.

Hendrix's depiction of Joe's defiance is bluster and his guitar wails in mockery. Mitchell's drumming is frenetic. Redding's guitar is deep and mournful. And with a figure made up of four rising notes from Hendrix, and a single crash of drum and guitar, the song is over.

In the instant of silence before the theatre was filled with cheers and wild applause, Marianne and I looked at each other. How could such a sinister song be so moving and so…beautiful? But it was. And, in this description all these years later, have I tried to disguise the hatefulness of the lyrics by finding in them an intimation of Joe's self-destruction? Perhaps, but the hatefulness of the lyrics does not lessen the effect the song had on both of us, nor our shared admiration of Hendrix.

Marianne says it took four days for her hearing to return to normal.

The second concert was by the Pink Floyd and was in the South of France just outside Saint Tropez. It took place in August 1970. Marianne and I were at the family house in Rocbaron, and we drove down the coast and found the site for the concert early in the evening, when it was still light. Hundreds of chairs were arranged on the floor of a small valley, an abandoned quarry perhaps, the shape of a U. The stage was in the base of the U, and the speakers had been placed on the clifftops behind the stage and along the sides of the U. People arrived.

The sky grew dark, lights were switched on, and the empty stage illuminated. We waited, and watched. The expectation built. And the group came on stage. There were no histrionics. They took up their positions, David Gilmour bending over his guitar, Nick Mason in his seat surrounded by drums and cymbals, Waters slipping the strap from his bass guitar over his head, and Rick Wright waiting at his two-decker keyboard. There was a single note from the keyboard, a chord played on the guitar, a brief rumble of bass guitar notes, and a light scatter of drumbeats, followed by silence. And then the Floyd played. One long piece after another, a concert of beautiful, challenging music played by a group at the height of their powers. The concert lasted late into the night.

Opinions differ on how to categorise the music played by the Floyd. It has been called hippie rock, psychedelic rock, progressive rock and, by people who have despaired of finding an appropriate genre, avantgarde music.

Oh, and yes, there were those mesmeric, nihilistic words, half sung and half whispered into the microphone.

One of the pieces played was 'A Saucerful of Secret'. If the Jimi Hendrix Experience started 'Hey Joe' in a controlled and structured way and gradually deconstructed the piece, the Pink Floyd did the opposite with 'A Saucerful of Secrets'. They moved from chaos to order.

They opened the piece with a drone from the bass guitar, and then immediate discord and pandemonium, with the repeated crash of cymbals, chaotic drumming and howling sounds from the lead guitar as Gilmour dragged his slide up and down the strings. Some febrile order was introduced by Mason as he settled into a rapidly repeated figure on his drums, which he played for minutes on end. The noise from the guitars and the keyboards continued, testing the nerves of the audience.

Waters abandoned his guitar and walked across the stage to a massive gong, hanging in a frame. He took hold of a huge drumstick of the kind timpanists use, and stood waiting, head bowed, his arm hanging straight, pulled down by the weight of the drumstick. Slowly he raised the drumstick and, when the cue came, he struck the gong with a massive blow and a rich sound rang out over the valley. Then he struck it again, and again, and again. The noise built to a point where I wondered if I could continue to bear it, and suddenly there was silence.

Through the silence, so to speak, came an organ chord, soft and comforting. Wright held the chord for a long time, letting it wash over us. He moved to another chord, and so to a sequence of chords, each held floating in the air for long moments, replacing the discord of the first part of the piece with familiar harmonies. And then Gilmour moved to a microphone, and joined the slow progression of organ chords with a wordless chant, holding each note for long moments, so that the chant sounded, for all the world, like a lament.

Marianne and I drove back to Rocbaron in silence.

Childbirth in London

Our daughter Alicia was born in 1970, and our son Frank in 1972. Both were born in London but, apart from that, each birth could not have been more different. Alicia was born in the private health system. It was winter. The hospital was a drab building dating from the Victorian era. Marianne's room looked down on a cemetery. The birth was by forceps. No one told me what was going on, let alone sought my advice. Marianne was given an anaesthetic, and was unconscious throughout the process.

And there was worse to come. Marianne woke to find that the baby had been born, but it was not in the room. She asked the first nurse who came into her room whether the baby was all right.

The nurse replied, 'I hope so.'

Marianne had to wait, in a mixture of exhaustion and distress, for another hour before being presented with Alicia and being allowed to hold her, and another couple of hours after that before a doctor, whom she had not seen before and did not see again, reassured her that Alicia was healthy and normal.

Both Marianne and I had intended having Alicia in the National Health system, but Marianne's mother put pressure on Marianne, in the form of a stream of distressed and sometimes angry phone calls, to use the private system. The stream of calls wore us down and, when Mathilde offered to pay for everything, we caved in. We had a GP whom we quite liked and who recommended an obstetrician. The obstetrician was annoyingly posh but, having met him, we felt obliged to go on with him. Of course, the money Marianne's mother sent us did not cover everything. And our nice GP turned up at the hospital, hung about to no purpose, and then billed us for two hours' consultation.

Our son Frank was born in the British public health system. It was summer. The windows of the hospital were large and the rooms full of light. The place bustled with activity. The nurses were accommodating. Marianne was having trouble following a pattern of breathing she had learnt, and so I lay on the bed beside her, doing the breathing too, while she concentrated on my mouth and followed my lead. When the time came to take her into the labour ward, they wheeled us in together, me still lying on the bed, Marianne with her eyes fixed on my mouth. Once in the ward, I was given covers for my shoes and a gown and cap. The lead nurse in the team put a chair next to the head of the bed, where I could hold Marianne's hand and continue to help her follow the pattern of breathing.

The labour ward consisted of a line of beds, with curtains that could be pulled around each one. There were two other women giving birth, and there were a couple of obstetricians, a man and a woman, wearing gowns, but evidently dressed under those gowns in the mad fashion – flared trousers, extravagant colours – of the times. They wandered cheerfully about, ready if needed.

I was allowed to stay throughout the birth, and was there to see Frank lifted into the air.

There was an excruciating moment when the trainee midwife cried out, 'He's so big. He's a monster!' And then, 'Oh my god, what have I said?'

But the laughter from the others reassured us. Frank was quickly swaddled and handed to Marianne, and then handed to me. It was four in the afternoon. The sunlight poured into the ward, and I had my second child in my arms.

When Marianne fell pregnant with Frank, we agreed that nothing would stop us using the public health service. We would not let ourselves be bullied by medicos. We would keep Mathilde at bay. And we would do some research into the whole business of childbirth. Both of us asked around, and a local librarian suggested that we read a book called *Birth* by Sheila Kitzinger.

Kitzinger argued that, if neither the mother nor the child was at risk, women should reject the medical model. Childbirth was normal and natural and not an illness, and they should take control of the process themselves. If they wanted to have the birth at home, then they should do so. If they wanted to have the child while they lay on the floor, or propped themselves up in a corner, or rolled about and screamed, or crawled around on all fours, they should do so.

Two pieces of good luck followed: Marianne went to a prenatal briefing at the hospital and came home to report that the doctor and the midwives at the briefing were open to the ideas of Kitzinger; and at a second meeting one of the midwives told her that Sheila Kitzinger ran classes at a centre in Marble Arch, just three stops on the Central underground line from where we lived. Marianne enrolled in a course with the enigmatic title of Psychosexual Prophylaxis.

Marianne came back from the first meetings of the course full of enthusiasm. Kitzinger, she said, was inspirational. The course, as the title vaguely indicated, was not just about preparing for childbirth. It was also about maintaining an active sex life during the pregnancy. All good. Most of the sessions were for the pregnant women, but one was for the partners as well, and so on the appointed evening Marianne and I entered the centre together.

The room where the course took place had no solid furniture. It was carpeted, there were a number of beanbags, and any number of cushions. Eight women, all of them large with child, lolled about on the beanbags or on cushions on the floor, or propped up against the wall. Their partners, shoeless, sat uneasily about. We were none too sure what we had let ourselves in for. Kitzinger entered, wearing loose trousers and a floppy kind of smock. I relaxed. She was a reassuring and kindly-looking person. She had a forceful presence but there was no sense of the fanatic about her.

What did I learn? Well, the breathing for one thing, and that we had rights. If I had not attended the course, I would not have dared lie down next to Marianne. We would not have insisted that I stay there as we were wheeled along the corridor. And I would not have had such a graphic understanding of the process of the baby leaving the womb.

Kitzinger asked us to come closer together so that she was facing us all. She took a bald-headed doll, and a small plastic bucket, and sat with her legs spread wide. She put the doll inside the bucket and placed the bucket between her legs. I could see now that the bottom of the bucket had been removed and replaced with foam rubber. Kitzinger then told us that the woman would push and the baby would emerge, the top of the head first, but then would retract. She had one hand inside the bucket and she pushed the doll forward. Now I could see a vertical slit in the foam rubber, which opened up slightly to show the top of the doll's skull.

Kitzinger explained that the woman should relax, and then push again. 'It might help if you cry out,' she said. 'It is your baby. You do not have to restrain yourself. Scream as loud as you like.' Kitzinger let out an unholy scream. 'Push again,' she said, and the doll's head appeared once again, a bit more of it this time, pushing the lips of the foam rubber vagina further apart. 'Breathe,' she said, and she breathed loudly in the pattern of short gasps and deep breaths that she had taught us. 'Scream as much you like,' she said, and she screamed again.

Now all our eyes were riveted on the doll's head. It withdrew and then more of it appeared. It withdrew, but not entirely. More noise, and the doll's head was completely out. One of the women screamed in sympathy. More breathing and shouting, and the doll popped out. People fell back into their beanbags or against the wall in relief. Some of the women were smiling as if they had given birth themselves there and then. One of the men was clutching a cushion as if he would never let it go.

Kitzinger said she wanted to finish the session by getting the women to experience something approximating the real pain they could expect. 'I want each of you men to pinch the inside of your partner's thigh,' she said. 'Do it gently.'

We all did so. The doll and the bucket had banished any modesty.

'Now, I want you to pinch harder.'

The room was filled with brief gasps and squeals of pain.

'A bit harder now,' Kitzinger said, and there were more gasps and squeals and whimpers of pain, some of them beginning to sound resentful.

'I want you to do this at home, so that you become used to the pain,' Kitzinger said.

I wondered at that. Doing it regularly might put a stress on the relationship at just the wrong time.

'Pinch once more,' Kitzinger said.

I made as if I was pinching but did not. Marianne looked gratefully at me.

'Enough,' Kitzinger said. 'Rub the spot where you have been pinching.'

The session ended with each man gently caressing the inside of his partner's thigh.

Testing parental love in Notting Hill Gate

It was early April 1972. We were living in a basement flat in Notting Hill Gate, London, and Marianne was six months pregnant.

In mid-evening. she began to have pains in her abdomen. They got worse. We hesitated until around midnight, when we began to panic. I called a doctor, who came and immediately arranged for an ambulance to take Marianne to hospital. I rang friends in desperation and they came and took Alicia, who was two and a bit, back to their place, and I climbed into the ambulance alongside Marianne.

At the hospital, nurses put Marianne on a mobile bed. She was in agony, but the nurses did nothing. I pleaded with them to give her something to relieve the pain but they explained that until she had been examined they could do nothing. Giving her a painkiller might relieve the pain, but it might also disguise the cause. I understood the logic but it was awful to see Marianne in such distress.

At last,the examination was done, and the problem was diagnosed as indigestion! The culprit, the examining doctor decided after talking to both of us, was probably a cucumber.

The doctor wanted to keep Marianne under observation for another day and night to make sure that her crisis had had no effect on the baby. I walked home at about eight a.m., having had no sleep at all, rang my friends and walked around to their flat to collect Alicia. I carried her back to our basement flat, and went in. I sat down.

Alicia ran off into her room, came back with a button she had found somewhere, and shoved it up her nose.

I leapt forward and grabbed her, but it was too late. I held her upside down and shook her (yes) but the button had gone right in. I looked up her nostril and could just see a bit of it, but there was no way I could reach it, particularly now that Alicia was struggling and screaming. There was a hospital nearer than Marianne's and I walked and ran, carrying Alicia, to the emergency department there.

After a long wait, a doctor examined Alicia, produced a sophisticated pair of tweezers from somewhere, and removed the button with nonchalant ease. He even held his tweezers with the button aloft, as if expecting applause from some unseen auditorium. There was paperwork to complete, and I was back in the street, carrying my daughter, after something like three hours at the hospital. It was now lunchtime and we went and had a pizza. Alicia was now in excellent spirits, and consumed an entire pizza by herself, to the audible amazement of a couple sitting at a nearby table. ('My god. Have you seen how much that little kid has eaten?') Alicia and I then took the bus to Marianne's hospital. Marianne was delighted to see Alicia and seemed uninterested when I told her about the button.

Time passed. Two months later, Marianne experienced labour pains right on schedule, went into the cucumber hospital, and Frank was brought into the world with reasonable ease. All was well except for the fact that he was born with jaundice and looked very yellow. As a result, Marianne and Frank were kept in hospital for a week.

On the day of Frank's birth I left the hospital about eight p.m., fetched Alicia from the same friends, fed her and put her to bed, undressed and got into bed myself, and fell into a deep sleep. From which I was woken by a small person standing alongside the bed and poking me in the cheek. I took Alicia into bed with me, settled her down and fell into an exhausted sleep again. From which I was woken by Alicia poking me in the other cheek. And so the night wore on. I would go to sleep and Alicia would wake me. I would fall asleep again and Alicia would wake me again.

I am no expert in child psychology, but I managed to work out for myself that with Marianne gone, Alicia was not going to let me go. Sleep was a little like going away, and so to reassure herself that I was still there, she would wake me up.

On the first morning after Frank's birth, I gave Alicia her breakfast at some very early hour, and then sat down to eat mine. I was sitting in our main room, munching on my cereal, when Alicia walked to the middle of the room, turned to face me and shoved something up her nose.

I leapt from my chair, dived across the room shouting, 'No, you bloody don't,' and grabbed her. I held her upside down and shook her (yes), and a small piece of folded paper popped out of her nose and fell to the floor.

I took Alicia with me to the hospital to see Marianne and Frank. Marianne was sitting up in bed looking wonderfully rested. Frank was in a bassinet next to the bed and already looking less yellow. Alicia was unaffected by her sleepless night, and overjoyed to see her mother.

The days passed. Each day, Marianne looked ever more rested, the proud and contented mother. Frank became a normal colour. Alicia was full of energy. And I was ever more an exhausted wreck.

When Marianne and Frank came home, I slept. Alicia woke me just once, and I took her in my arms and cuddled her. She lay still on my tummy for several wonderful moments, and then wriggled free from my embrace with that sudden energy little children have, and I slept on.

An ecumenical baptism in the village of Rocbaron

Frank was born in mid-June 1972, and we decided his baptism should take place in late July in Rocbaron, when a good part of the French tribe would be gathered on holiday there. My dad was on a trip to Europe, his first outing from Australia since my mother died, and he was going to be there too.

The extended family and some hangers-on assembled for Frank's baptism on a Tuesday morning in the small village square, with its small church, its small, unexceptional fountain, and its obligatory plane tree. We made a sartorially diverse group. Marianne and her sister Laetitia already had deep summer tans. They stood side by side, two splendid French women, Marianne in a floral patterned dress of bright yellows on a dark navy blue background, Laetitia in a vibrant red dress that reached down to her ankles. Both had long, lustrous black hair. My mother-in-law Mathilde was dressed in a dark green satiny outfit, and rattled a little with jewellery. My brother-in-law Jean-Claude was in fawn trousers, white shoes and a loose-fitting white collarless shirt, open some way down his chest. Our nephews and niece were dressed in a variety of clothing and colours better suited to hanging around the swimming pool. My father-in-law Achille was in an off-white linen suit, and my dad was in the dark grey suit and black lace-up shoes he always wore in Sydney. He had replaced his tie with his clerical collar. He was holding Frank, and looking as pleased as punch.

I sported the fashion of early 1970s London: jeans so flared that they hid my shoes entirely, a darkish blue linen jacket, hair down to and over the collar, sideburns down to the jawline, and my truly awful paisley shirt in which orange dominated and which I had worn when I told the world's longest joke. I was holding Alicia. She was still tiny enough to sit on my forearm and dangle her legs down between my arm and my chest, so that she was looking straight at my face, and I could nuzzle her cheek. She was wearing a navy blue dress with large white dots, made more vivid in the sunlight.

And there was a priest, in a long cream and white robe. This was not the village priest but a Parisian one, invited by Mathilde to officiate at both the baptism and the accompanying mass. And of course he was glad to, in exchange for a day or two staying with us before the event and a day or two afterwards. There is no such thing as a free sacrament.

It was at this point that the first glitch occurred. The village priest was not there, and the church doors were locked. Some locals had turned up, and we asked them what we should do. Wait, they said. It was not uncommon for the village priest to be late. But he always turned up, eventually. We milled about for a bit, with my military father-in-law, a stickler for punctuality, growing visibly irritated. The village priest arrived some ten minutes late. He was dressed from head to toe in black, adding another element to the sartorial variation of the assembled company. He opened the church, we all trooped in, and proceedings started.

The baptism went off without a hitch, with the village priest doing the business and the Parisian priest in attendance. I was a little surprised since I had understood from Mathilde that the Parisian priest would be officiating. But no matter. All had gone well.

Problems arose as we moved to the mass. Both priests moved towards the altar, and the village priest appeared to elbow his way ahead. There was a touch of medieval symbolism in a figure in white and a figure in black doing a discreet bit of pushing and shoving in front of the altar, and more than a touch of symbolism in the fact that the one in white lost. The Parisian priest looked profoundly irritated, and then embarrassed at having displayed an unchristian sentiment so openly. He stood aside and the village priest took charge. The village priest spoke too loudly for the intimate surroundings, possibly to counter a tendency to slur some of the longer words, but, apart from that, he carried off the mass with the required solemnity.

We flowed out of the church, stood about for a short while, and then drifted back to the house, where Achille uncorked some bottles of champagne, and we drank a toast to Frank. (Dad had a glass of juice.) The village priest and the other villagers who had come in for the champagne left, and the household sat down under a plane tree in the garden for lunch.

A few days earlier, when we were talking about the event, Dad had said he would like to conduct a small, very informal ceremony later in the day, and it had been agreed that everyone would gather in the salon of the house at five p.m. I sensed that one or two of my extended family were excited at the prospect of seeing what a Protestant minister might do. Would he raise his voice and stab the air with his finger like Robert Mitchum in *The Night of the Hunter?* Would he go into a trance? Would he sing, and wave his hands back and forth above his head, like those happy-clappy gatherings you see from time to time on TV?

Five p.m. came. Some twelve of us gathered in a rough circle in the salon, sitting on a mixture of sofas and chairs. Dad cradled Frank in his arms and, with Marianne as interpreter, gave an extempore prayer welcoming Frank into the world and wishing him a happy and fulfilled life. I could see the delight in the Parisian priest's eyes. Dad then handed Frank to me, and began saying a few words to both Marianne and me about our responsibilities to our children.

I am not sure who among us had let slip to the village priest that there would be this extra ceremony in the afternoon, but he was suddenly outside the house, banging on the front door. Dad stopped talking, and the village priest began shouting, demanding to be let in. Jean-Claude went into the small corridor leading to the front door. By now, the village priest was banging on one of the windows and pressing his face against the glass. Jean-Claude, normally a man of some authority, opened the front door and the village priest charged past him, stumbled down the single step from the corridor into the salon, and lurched towards us. The Parisian priest was clearly mortified. The Catholic Church was not scrubbing up too well in the presence of his Protestant colleague. He stood up and tried to quieten his Catholic colleague down. It took him a moment to get the village priest's attention, but he did, and the village priest fell silent. He looked around the room, and appeared to realise for the first time that the ceremony was already under way. The Parisian priest made room for the village priest on his sofa, and the village priest sat down heavily. He muttered and snorted for a moment, and then his head dropped on to his chest.

Dad looked at Marianne. She nodded, and he continued. He wound up his advice to Marianne and me, and said that he would leave us with a short reading from the gospel. He opened his Bible, removed a bookmark, and read for not much more than a minute. He made a short comment, paused, and raised his right hand, with two fingers extended, to give the benediction. At that moment, the village priest came alive. He jumped up and announced that all three priests should pronounce the benediction together. He motioned to Dad to stop, pulled him across the circle to stand next to him, and then turned and tried to drag the Parisian priest to his feet. The Parisian priest resisted, and the village priest tugged harder. Dad in turn was embarrassed for the village priest and tried to restrain him. For a moment, we were treated to all three clerics engaged in some kind of struggle. It was not up to the standards of an all-out bar room brawl, but the fact that all three participants were men of the cloth made it out of the ordinary.

Cross-cultural table manners

Dad spent a week with us at *un petit coin de paradis*, before going to see friends in Switzerland. The baptism was early in the week but he was subjected to another culturally rich event before he left.

Each summer, when the family was assembled in full force at *un petit coin de paradis* and in holiday mood, we would prepare, cook and eat a major dish. The dish might be paella, or a bouillabaisse or, in this case, couscous. When fully prepared, the dish would be carried into the garden, photographed extensively and then eaten by the whole family at the stone table under the plane tree.

When we took our places, Mathilde assumed the head of the table and Dad was placed on her right. I was placed next to Dad to keep him company. Mathilde was excited. She had spent the first twenty-three years of her life in Algeria and this dish was the dish of her childhood. Now she was shouting (or speaking very loudly, if you will), as she spooned a copious amount of grain into her mouth. Lesser mortals might have stopped speaking while eating, but not Mathilde. This meant that her first mouthful of the couscous grain was sprayed over the table in front of her and some of it over Dad. Dad flinched for a moment and then realised that flinching would appear rude and so he sat in a storm of couscous, making a valiant effort to look as if all were perfectly normal.

And again, I remain unsure whether Dad broadened his Australian accent on purpose, or whether it was some kind of defence, but in a lull in the storm he leant over to me and said, 'Might I be mistaken but aren't the manners a bit rough here today?'

Again, I need to be careful. The way in which my parents-in-law, my brother-law and sister-in-law, and my proliferation of nieces and nephews fell upon the couscous was not poor table manners. It was the highest of praise.

Contributing to international goodwill

In 1973, there was an international furore over the French nuclear tests in the Pacific. The tests were atmospheric. Greenpeace had sailed vessels into the testing zone. France was in the process of ignoring an International Court of Justice ruling that they cease testing. There was fear and loathing in the Pacific-rim countries and beyond.

In the summer of 1973, Marianne, Alicia three, Frank one, and I drove to Dover, took a ferry to Calais nd drove to Paris. We stayed there for a couple of nights, and then headed off to the family house in the south for our summer holidays. To get there, we drove overnight. I slept for three hours in the afternoon before we left. We packed the car, settled the kids in the back, and set off at about ten in the evening. At that time, the traffic out of Paris was manageable. Once on the motorway, the traffic was light and the driving was easy. At about two a.m., we pulled into a rest area. I ate something, slept for about an hour, and then drove on. We arrived at the family house late morning. I unpacked the car, changed into swimming trunks, descended from our attic bedroom to the garden and dived into the swimming pool.

At least that was my intention, but there was a man in the garden, dressed elegantly for the summer in a light blue shirt, white trousers, and boating shoes.

He rose from his chaise longue, and greeted me in a heavily accented but grammatically impeccable English. 'You must be Michael.'

'Yes, I am. And you are...?'

'My name is Alain Bogart. But you can call me Humphrey. Many people do. I am an old friend of your father-in-law.'

We shook hands, and I said, 'I hope you don't mind but I'm going to jump into the swimming pool. I've just driven overnight from Paris and need something to keep me awake through lunch.'

'Paris? I assume it was deserted. It always is once the vacation starts. Nothing is going on there.'

Something had been niggling me since we arrived in Paris, and now I snapped, 'Plenty is happening in the rest of the world.'

'That is to say...?'

'I'm saying that on the other side of the world there are riots and demonstrations against the French. The English papers were full of it when we left five days ago but bugger me if I could find any mention of it in the Parisian papers.'

'Ah...'

'It's shocking. It's as if no one here gives a damn about the environmental issues, or the health of people in the Pacific-rim countries. The disregard for the island nations like Tonga and Vanuatu is breath-taking.' I could hear a terrible whine coming into in my voice, and I stopped. I took a deep breath. 'Look,' I said. 'You have to excuse me. I'm tired and I've forgotten my manners.'

'But please.'

'No. I apologise. Really, I do. I shouldn't hold you responsible for something your government does. It is the most unjustified thing to do.'

Alain Bogart was smiling. 'I understand. Off you go for your swim. I am sure we will talk some more.'

The swimming pool was further down the long garden, and I headed there and dived in. The swim, and venting my anger on poor old Humphrey Bogart, had calmed me down, and when I climbed out I felt much better. I went upstairs and dressed for lunch, and came downstairs and into the garden again. Bogart was no longer there but my mother-in-law was.

She greeted me and said, in French, 'We have an old friend staying here, Admiral Bogart. You will like him. He speaks English very well. He and your father-in-law were in the naval college together.' She paused, and then, as if I would be pleased to hear the following information, she went on, 'Admiral Bogart played an important part in choosing the Mururoa islands for the nuclear testing program.'

Up against the authority in inner London

From 1971 to 1979, I was a community education worker for an adult education institute in inner London. The institute provided non-credit courses for the people in the areas of Shepherds Bush and White City.

My job was to take educational services to community groups on the institute's patch. For example, I set up an arts and crafts club for parents and children on a big public housing estate, a support group for people who were out of work, a training course for volunteers working on a welfare rights stall in Shepherds Bush market, and short taster courses for busy people and people who had never previously darkened our doors.

It was satisfying work, but I must admit that I had the most fun setting up new courses in the institute's formal program. As long as people turned up, I had virtual carte blanche. And so I set up courses on rock music, black power, civil liberties, alternative societies, alternative education, science fiction, women's liberation, our planet, welfare rights… In the institute's brochure, we assembled this eclectic bunch of courses under the unhelpful title of Special Studies.

In early 1972, I learnt that the South London Gay Liberation Front (GLF) had approached the Inner London Education Authority (ILEA) with a proposal for a gay studies course and had been knocked back. I contacted the South London GLF and said I would help them try again. Within the context of our Special Studies, I was pretty sure we would have no trouble placing a course on gay issues.

I met the president of the South London GLF. We discussed the nature of the course (an analysis of the legal, political and social challenges gay people faced), and drafted a blurb to put in the institute's prospectus. The blurb stated that the course would put the gay point of view and all the speakers would be gay.

I included the course in the institute's program due to start in September 1972. Time passed, with nary a squeak from the authority, and we sent the institute's prospectus to the printer, carrying the news that, in amongst courses on keep fit, dressmaking, holiday French, and the novels of Jane Austen, we were offering a course under the single-word title of Homosexuality.

During the summer break, the authority, like some massive dinosaur, stirred, and disgorged a three-line letter saying that we could not run the course and that it was the policy of the authority not to support 'sectarian groups with particular beliefs, attitudes or ways of life'. This was nonsense. Our very own institute ran courses in conjunction with the Christian community, a centre following the teachings of Rudolf Steiner. But the letter mentioned homosexuals and so its interpretation of 'sectarian' went wider than the religious one. What about our black studies course in which all the speakers were black? What about our course on women's liberation, in which all the speakers were active in the women's movement?

I talked it over with Marianne, and decided to fight.

I shall not go into detail. There were exchanges of letters with the authority, meetings, petitions, pleadings, I wrote a paper on what was and what was not propaganda. At one meeting with senior people from the authority, the principal of my institute told the group that I went to a large laundry two mornings a week to run an English language class for the Asian women there. 'Now that's what you should be doing,' one of the senior officers exclaimed.

The crunch came. I had talked to the Guardian newspaper, and they had contacted the authority's press office, and been told that the decision to withdraw the course had been made at the local level. This time I wrote a letter to the Guardian, and delivered it together with a copy of the authority's letter refusing the course. The journalist tore a strip off the authority's press people for lying to him, and the paper printed a sarcastic story in its education section under the title of 'The Lost Course', quoting the authority's letter of refusal in full.

I was immediately in terrible odium. The principal of the institute called me into his office, where we had a frank exchange of views. I wandered around the office like a marked man and, sure enough, a letter arrived in which the authority summoned me, in the company of my principal, to a formal meeting at County Hall, the massive building on the other side of the Thames from the Palace of Westminster.

On the eve of my interview, in the best Thurberesque tradition, I took to my bed with a high temperature, and in the morning I felt far from well. I took a taxi, but we got caught up in a traffic jam and I was forced to quit the taxi, dive into the Underground, and make a dash across Westminster Bridge on foot. I arrived at the appointed room in County Hall with about thirty seconds to spare. The room had oak panelling and a horrid, formal feel to it. Two senior officers sat on one side of a heavy table. The chairs for my principal and me were set a little back from the other side of the table.

I said very little at the outset of the meeting but, some ten minutes in, one of the officers described my actions as 'unworthy', and I had drawn my chair up to the table and was suddenly talking. Rash, insubordinate, unwise, perhaps. Unworthy, no. Appoint people to experiment, then you are going to have to support them. Ask them to go through the task of identifying and defining their community, then you cannot make a unilateral redefinition of the concept in order to suit some comfortable central policy. (Can you hear my voice rising?) Women are part of the community and have a right to meet and, with our help, to look for ways to combat sexism. Black people are part of our community and have a perfect right to have a course in which black speakers put the black point of view. Gay people are part of our community – ten per cent according to some estimates – and they have rights too.

I finished, breathless and sweating, and the two officers and my principal looked at me in silence. I looked at each in turn, with what I felt were slightly crazed eyes. One of the officers then read some paragraphs from a staff code that I had never read, or seen, or even heard of before. I was asked to acknowledge that I had understood what had been read out to me.

I said, 'Yes.'

Despite the formality of these final moments, I felt the two officers were more amiably disposed towards me. At the very least, I had demonstrated that I was not motivated by a fatuous desire to stir up trouble. My principal and I left the room, and in the corridor outside, he said I had just completed the first step towards my dismissal. I had caused him a lot of grief, and I could understand why his tone was less forgiving than that of the officers. I went home to bed.

In a classic bureaucratic move, the ILEA set up a working party to look at 'an educational response to controversial learning situations'. The working party, of which I was a member, met several times over the next twelve months, and a report was circulated. In that time, I set about organising the gay studies course again. I had to do it under the close scrutiny of my principal, and submit it to the institute's newly established academic board. All this was done and, with a bowdlerised version of the original blurb and the underwhelming title Homosexuality: Changing Attitudes, the course was advertised to start in September 1974, two years after our previous attempt. We had lost the militancy implicit in a public association with the Gay Liberation Front, but the basic principle was maintained: this was a course in which gay people would put a gay point of view.

The course comprised six two-hour meetings over consecutive Wednesday evenings. An inspector from the ILEA sat exuding disapproval through the first meeting, inhibiting everyone. By the following Monday, he had circulated a report recommending the course be closed forthwith. He said that the course was a discussion group 'set up by homosexual groups', and that the discussions were directed towards confirming homosexuals in their attitudes and gaining public acceptance for their views. On all that, he was right. He also said that the group was made up largely, if not entirely, of homosexuals. On that, he was wrong. At the final session, people volunteered information on their own sexual preferences. Eight were gay, and nine were not. Of those who were not, some had children or siblings or friends who were.

The principal of the institute, who was now back on side, attended the second meeting and wrote a counter-report. He and the vice principal attended the third meeting, and it was only when they left that the course came alive. At last, people could say a little about themselves and begin the exchanges that provide the magic in adult education. At the fifth meeting, a criminologist presented a paper on labelling theory and societal definitions of deviance. She chose to present the paper in a coldly professional manner. But she knew what she was doing, because the discussion that followed was long and heartfelt.

On the final evening, people were encouraged to talk about their reasons for attending. One woman's response put all the alarums and excursions into perspective. She said that she always went to an adult education class on Wednesday evenings, and amongst the courses on offer on Wednesday that autumn, this one on homosexuality had looked the most interesting.

On a beach at Rye

My first role in university student theatre was the sergeant of police in a production of Gilbert and Sullivan's *Pirates of Penzance*. The year was 1960. It was a rocky old production, but the sergeant's songs went down well. A week later, the director of the next year's university revue contacted me. He wanted me to do a trial run in a lunchtime revue he was organising for the first week (orientation week) of the next academic year.

I was given a monologue in which I was a photographer complaining about my job. The monologue was full of gross double entendres. For example, I complained about cockroaches chewing on my equipment while I was taking a photo. Awful. But the crowd roared with laughter.

I tell you this because I experienced something that many actors experience early in their careers. It is the magical moment when they feel that they have the audience in the palm of their hand and that, with a cocked eyebrow, or a shrug, or the flick of a finger, they can make the audience laugh or cry. From that moment, they are hooked and they go in search of the same experience for the rest of their lives. Some have the experience again and again. Others are still playing bit parts thirty or forty years down the track, and hoping against hope.

Over my remaining two years at university, I played in a number of productions including those revues. I made people laugh but I did not experience that magical moment again.

I got to London in mid-1963, and in early 1964 a group of us decided to stage an intimate revue. I had thought I would limit my involvement to writing a couple of sketches, but, somehow, I found myself in the cast. Once that had happened, the hope that I would have that magical moment took hold again.

The show was a flop. We performed for three weeks in a pretty little theatre called the Lyric Hammersmith, and on one Saturday matinee there were fewer people in the audience (seven) than in the cast (eight). On one evening, and I do not know why, the theatre was almost full. I had two monologues, and people laughed out loud during both. It was gratifying, but the sense of having absolute control was not there.

At the end of the season, a theatrical agent approached me and offered to take me onto his books. This sounds wonderful, but the agent was starting out and no older than me. He said he could find me auditions, but I hated the demeaning process of auditions. What I wanted was an agent who would find me roles without my having to audition and that, of course, was impossible for an unknown.

And the backstage atmosphere in the revue had been unpleasant. The cast split into two distinct groups: those who considered themselves real actors; and the rest of us. We all had our union cards, but those of us from the Sydney University days had got them by forming a company, and then employing ourselves. The others had earned their cards the hard way, working in repertory theatre in the provinces.

And so I came to one of those crossroads in life. I was in my twenties. I could do anything. I was already toying with the idea of moving on from the UK and spending some time in the Caribbean. The theatre looked like hard work. And if the backstage bickering was anything to go by, I would find myself working with some difficult people. I chose not to go on the agent's books, and I have often wondered, 'What if?'

On a Friday night eight years later, Marianne and I were sitting chatting in our Notting Hill Gate flat when the phone rang. I answered and Bruce Beresford identified himself. He was on the rise in the film industry.

'Look, Mike, I begin shooting a film next week and one of the main characters has just dropped out. Are you still a member of Actors' Equity?'

'Yes.'

'Good. Can you get the next six weeks off work?'

'I can try.'

'I need you to play the part of Curly.'

Bruce was making a sequel to a film I had seen, and I said, 'I don't look anything like Curly. I've got straight hair and I wear glasses.'

'That's all right. We can change the name of the character to Four-eyes Fenton.'

The next Tuesday, I was picked up at four a.m. and driven to the coast near Rye, where I was dressed, made up, and asked to step in front of the camera. Behind the camera were about thirty people: script people, continuity people, boom holders, grips, sound technicians, the camera man, the camera operator, the focus puller, lighting technicians, money people, the director, the first assistant director, the second assistant director...the whole professional shebang.

And there I was, on the other side of the invisible line, alone, and holding a short rope attached to the muzzle of a camel.

'This,' I thought to myself, 'is the last time.'

PS: In early 1978, I was having a drink in the bar of the Riverside Studios Arts Centre in Hammersmith, and a man greeted me. He was one of the real actors who had been in that revue fourteen years earlier. He looked a bit beaten-down. We chatted. He was still acting. It had been tough but he had been in a successful show for three nights in Brighton a fortnight ago, and he was doing this show in Riverside Studios. It was a series of readings, nothing much, but I should have seen the gig in Brighton. The people loved it.

'Do you have a partner?' I asked him.

'Oh, you know how it is. Not at the moment.'

'Children?'

'I haven't had the time!'

His name came back to me. It was Guy.

'Where do you live, Guy?'

'I've got a flat in Highgate. Well, it's not really a flat, more a bedsitter, but it's got lots of light. I'm happy there. And you?'

'A house, well, a small terrace, but it's ample enough for my partner and me, and our two ankle-biters.'

He laughed. We chatted a bit longer, and then I made my excuses and walked home to Marianne and the kids.

A mural in a Shepherd's Bush basement

The patch of the adult education institute where I worked during the 1970s included a part of the London borough of Hammersmith, and in 1976, through contacts on the borough council, I heard of a group of blind people who had been given a lease on an unoccupied house. The leader of the group was a tall Scot, a former journalist of about forty, now blind. He had talked money out of various authorities, talked the house out of the council and, with the help of a bunch of enthusiasts, set up the Hammersmith Self-Help Centre for the Blind and Partially Sighted. He was interested when I made contact. Through me, he could get a couple more Braillers, but I suggested we could do more than that. We could set up a program of Braille classes, and the adult education institute would publicise the program and pay the tutor.

At an in-service training day, I mentioned my institute's relationship with the self-help centre and was contacted by an inspector who said she would like to pay the centre a visit. The centre's director and I set up the visit for a late afternoon and evening, so that the inspector could see a Braille class in progress, attend a discussion group, and then join some people for a drink in the basement.

The inspector seemed genuinely impressed. She lingered in the class and the discussion group, and we went downstairs to the basement at about eight.

The basement was the biggest single space in the building, the floor area comprising the full width and depth of the main structure of the house. There were seven people present, conversing with a young man who was putting the final touches to a mural.

The mural covered one of the party walls. It was multicoloured and multi-textured. The colours were strong in places, and subtle and light in others. The texture consisted of fabrics of differing character, from silk to hessian, plastics, polystyrene and cardboard. The artist, whose name was Tyrone, worked at the mural energetically, with his back to us for most of the time, swinging round every now and then and looking down for a brush or a piece of material or a pot of paste, talking enthusiastically and explaining how he wanted the mural to work as a tactile or visual experience, or both, for the blind, the sighted, and people with every kind and degree of sight in between.

The director told us that Tyrone had been an art student.

I am not sure how the next piece of information came out. Did the inspector comment on the urgency with which Tyrone appeared to be working. Did I? Did the director, unprompted, explain? I do remember Tyrone turning and looking at us – at me, because I felt isolated in his regard at that moment whether he looked directly at me or not – and my understanding that there was something wrong about his eyes and my being told that, yes, he was eager to get the job finished because he was going blind.

The inspector and I left the centre after nine. She drove away and I walked to a telephone box and rang Marianne. She had just got in from teaching an evening class but she walked out of the house again, got back into our car, picked me up and took me to a pub in West Kensington.

Thinkers of one sort and another – Karl Marx, Jean-Paul Sartre, Thich Nhat Hanh – have wanted to make available heightened forms of consciousness which the rest of us may sometimes want to avoid. Alcohol can provide an escape, but not always. The speech may slow, but an undisciplined reflection rattles the mind. To stop thinking, I need a bad movie or loud music.

The Kensington Tavern in Elsham Road was a straightforward drinking house at the time, bare floorboards, and a venue for talented rock bands. We walked through the door and into a wall of sound. I ordered our drinks by mouthing the words, and we moved through the crowd towards the band.

If this were fiction, a short story, I would describe the hero standing, his wife's arm linked with his, holding his beer, staring at the rock band, surrounded by sound, tears running down his cheeks as he wept publicly but unnoticed for Tyrone, and for what he had seen in Tyrone's regard:

We have no control over our past. We can use it, interpret it, learn from it and even rewrite it, but the fact of it mockingly remains. Tyrone had been an art student. We have no guaranteed control over our future. We can try to influence it by learning, planning and taking action, but events happen that can divert the whole course of our lives. Tyrone's sight began failing. Our futures are there to haunt us. We may grow old. We will die. In this case, in a few months' time, Tyrone was going to be blind. Our pasts direct us forward, while obvious futures rush back to meet us, and others wait unseen, like footpads in a dark alley, to waylay us. All we have is the present, a moment in which we can make choices, in which we can either give in to our pasts or face up to some, at least, of our futures. Tyrone, in an act of defiance, made a mural!

In the real-life version, however, the memory I have is of standing completely engaged in the sight and the sound. The band was good. The drummer laid down a careering thunder of rhythms, stating the structures. The bass guitarist offered background comment in rich single notes, linking the drumming to the melodies of the lead guitar and the support guitar. Through a series of solos, instrumental duets and songs, the guitarists told their stories. After one particular song, the lead guitarist stepped away from the microphone and, with the rest of the group in support, began a long, rising, silvery solo. He played with no extraneous dramatics, moving a pace forward on the small stage, head bowed over the guitar, a professional in full control of his moment.

I was exhilarated and suddenly very tired. We went home.

I asked after Tyrone at the centre. He had finished the mural and then gone off the radar. I saw the mural as a one-finger salute to the Fates, and I like to think Tyrone took that attitude with him wherever he went.

Dressmaking against racism in Shepherd's Bush

In 1973, a woman called Mrs Jennings approached the London adult education institute where I worked. She was the secretary of 'a black women's league' in Shepherd's Bush.

Mrs Jennings was clear about how we could help. 'Our numbers are down,' she said. 'We need a well-organised activity around which we can build up our other activities. We have a sewing circle that meets once a week. Can you provide us with a professional teacher and turn it into a proper dressmaking class?'

'If the institute supports your group,' I said, 'we would like to think that the class was open to anyone, black or white.'

'Of course,' Mrs Jennings said, and then added after a pause, 'We are not a racist organisation.'

I already liked Mrs Jennings, and that was confirmed when I visited the hall, and met her face to face. She was a no-nonsense person, who went after what she considered her due, but no more. So we agreed that I would find four machines, and a tutor. She would find two other machines. I offered to waive the fees for the first term of the course, but Mrs Jennings insisted on paying the fees from the women's league coffers. She would let the group know this and they could pay their fees into the league's coffers, or not, depending on their circumstances.

'We are not a charity,' she said sternly. 'Nor are we an unfeeling business.'

We shook hands and I left.

None of our regular dressmaking tutors was available, so I referred to the panel of approved tutors held at County Hall, and they supplied me with the name and address of a tutor living a couple of streets away from the hall used by the women's league. I wrote to her, she replied, and I arranged to pick her up at her home and take her to meet the women's league committee.

The woman who opened the door was in her middle thirties, charming-looking, quietly spoken…and black. I drove her to the church hall very slowly. What would the women's league think? Would they assume that I had gone to a great deal of trouble to find them a black, as opposed to a white, tutor? Would they think that no white tutor had been willing to take the job on? Would they see my providing them with a black tutor as an unthinking act of racism?

We got to the hall and the tutor met Mrs Jennings and some of the committee. There was some slight trouble with accents at first since the tutor was Nigerian and the committee members were from the West Indies. But the encounter seemed to go well. I offered to drive the tutor home, but she said she would walk.

As soon as the tutor had left, Mrs Jennings turned and looked at me. Her regard was not warm. 'How did you choose that woman?' she asked.

'She's on the panel of approved tutors. I got her name and address from County Hall.'

'Did you choose her because she's black?'

'No.'

Mrs Jennings looked at me for a moment. 'She seems very suitable,' she said. And for the first time in our encounter, she smiled.

1980s

Unnoticed in Hanwell

I lived for nearly twenty years in the UK, and, in my final four years there, I was the warden of the Working Men's College in Camden, London. In that post, I was responsible for a full-time staff of twelve people, some hundred and forty part-time teachers, and a program of evening classes attended every week by hundreds of adult students.

Shortly after my appointment, a student in his mid-sixties called Gerry Webb cornered me in my office. He told me that he ran a series of talks at the Hanwell public library, held on the second Tuesday of the month. He had a vacant slot in November and could he book me as the speaker? I was flattered, and agreed.

'Excellent,' he said. 'Now I need a title.'

'Whatever happened to 1968?'

Gerry looked mystified.

'That's the title of my talk,' I said. '1968 was a year of upheaval and promise, but the promise has not been fulfilled. I want to examine why.'

Hanwell is a former village overtaken by urban sprawl, on the western fringes of London. I pulled up outside the library on the appointed date shortly before seven p.m. I had given myself lots of time but had got lost for more than twenty minutes in row upon row of identical brick and pebble-dash houses. The library building was small – the former village hall perhaps – and dark. I went up the steps and peered through a glass panel in the front door but could see no light. I knocked, and Gerry emerged from the murk, unlocked the door, let me in, and locked the door behind me. He led me into the business part of the library, and indicated a small table and two chairs between two library stacks.

Seated between the stacks were the people who had come to hear me talk. If you counted Gerry, there were six. Two were still wearing their overcoats, and showed no signs of taking them off.

Gerry and I sat down at the table. It was four minutes to seven p.m., and so we waited, ears cocked for a knock on the door. None came, and at seven p.m. Gerry stood, introduced himself, introduced me, and repeated the title of my talk. I got the impression that he was still mystified. Alarm bells should have rung but they did not.

I stood up, felt ridiculous, and sat down again. I started with the words, 'Of course, 1968 was a very special year, because that was the year when I got married.' There was no laughter. Well, it was a small crowd.

I reminded my audience of the cultural and political agitation that took place in 1968 – rock concerts in Hyde Park, hippies, the burgeoning underground press, demonstrations outside the US embassy against the war in Vietnam, and the civil rights marches in Northern Ireland. I recalled the demonstrations and struggle in other countries – the overturned cars and barricades in Paris, the all-too-brief flowering of freedom in what was then Czechoslovakia, the days of rioting in Chicago, and the student unrest that spread across the globe.

It was a year of disruption, I said, and it was also a year of hope. There was a belief that a more loving, more communal, less competitive life was possible.

I paused. No one spoke and so I posed the rhetorical question in my talk's title. What happened to 1968? Why did the sense of promise dissipate so quickly?

My audience remained mute, as did those alarm bells.

I went on. I believed, I said, that it was the troubles in Northern Ireland that sowed the seeds of doubt in the minds of people pursuing alternative and radical policies. The troubles there cast a shadow over the whole of the UK. People held back because they were aware that in one part of the country small but terrible minorities might take up their ideas.

I paused yet again, and yet again no one spoke. And so I told them that I had witnessed a small alternative London newspaper founder on the issue of Northern Ireland in the early 1970s. Violence was on the increase in Ulster and, in accordance with its stated policy, the paper reported not on the violence of the bloody-minded factions – that was covered in the mainstream press – but on the methods used by the British army in dealing with these factions. Having apparently taken sides, the paper began attracting sinister people into its office. There were disagreements within the staff on editorial policy. The Northern Ireland coverage lost readers who hankered after a comfortable extension of the underground press of the 1960s. The paper ran into financial trouble, and closed.

I found that I was standing. I sat down. Gerry stood, and called for comments. There was silence again, but Gerry waited.

Finally, one of the two women in the audience spoke. 'I think that we all remember the year we got married.'

Gerry wrapped proceedings up. He unlocked the library doors to let us all out, thanked me on the steps, and we parted company. I got into my car. What I had seen as momentous times had passed unnoticed in Hanwell. I drove back into central London, passing about Ealing through some kind of gateway from Hanwell's brick and pebble-dash universe back into mine.

PS: And now that I think about it, a good number of those brick and pebble-dash houses would have been mortgaged to the hilt, and their occupants too preoccupied with surviving to pay much attention to the children of the middle classes cavorting in the long summer grass, and singing, 'All you need is love'.

Averting disaster in London

The Working Men's College may sound like pretty small beer, but no matter how big or small an organisation is, if you are the CEO, then you are the person held responsible – for everything.

Two months after I accepted the job and a month before I actually began, the roof of the five-storey Edwardian building was badly damaged by fire. It meant that I was immediately dealing with loss adjusters, architects, heritage authorities, and one of the few building firms that had the necessary crafts to rebuild the roof and cupola.

Towards the end of the work on the roof, the college building manager – an old-time cockney – knocked on my office door and said, 'I fink you should come darn 'n' 'ave a look at the boiler room, guvner.'

Which I did, and saw that a large section of the boiler room ceiling had come away, revealing sheets of crumblng asbestos.

Two classical studies teachers burst into my office, stood toe to toe in front of my desk, and shouted blue murder at each other.

A maths teacher didn't turn up for classes, and late in the evening a colleague and I went to her address. We received no response when we knocked, and so we kicked the door in and found her on the floor where she had lain for two days, disabled by a stroke.

I thought the problems must slacken off a bit, but they never did, and I began to understand that most management is crisis-management. Constant, hectic reaction is the norm.

Classes at the college finished by nine thirty p.m. and the bar closed around ten thirty. I was working in my office shortly after ten thirty when a college student popped his head around my door.

'Good evening, warden,' he said.

'Good evening.'

'If you have a moment, you might look in on the small common room,' he said.

The small common room was at the end of a corridor beyond the larger common room and the bar. It was used for college council meetings, and by a few chess players, but often remained empty throughout the evening.

'Oh,' I said.

'Yes, you might want to pop your head in.'

'I'm nearly finished here. I'll go down there in a moment.'

'Good. I'm on my way out.'

'Thank you. Goodnight.'

'Goodnight, warden.'

I had lived and worked in the UK for eighteen years, but could still fail to appreciate the English understatement. 'If you have a moment... You might want...' And why had the student been so keen to tell me he was leaving? It had taken a moment or two but now I was worried. I abandoned the note, walked quickly down the corridor, and pushed open the common room door.

A woman in her twenties was sitting on a chair in the centre of the room, looking down at the floor. There were lighted candles on several of the tables. As I entered the room, something crushed under my shoes and I saw that the room was decorated with lines of coffee powder and white sugar.

'Hello,' I said but received no response. 'Are you celebrating something?' I asked.

Again, there was no response.

I brought a chair from one of the other tables and sat down. I kept my distance so as not to confront her, and from this position I could see a tin of lighter fluid under the table and within her easy reach.

We sat in the candlelight. What was I to do? I could reach for the lighter fluid, but would the young woman prevent me? I could go to the common room door, where I could look down the corridor in the hope of attracting someone's attention and still see the young woman if she moved…but the building felt very empty. I could go back to my office and ring for help, but would the young woman start a fire while I was out of the room? I could try talking some more, but I had no training in this. I could take hold of her, and try to restrain her, but then what? Charges of sexual assault? Or I could sit there, through the night, and do whatever I had to do if the young woman reached for the lighter fluid. Mrs Clarry, the lead cleaner, would appear at six or thereabouts the next morning. I decided on inaction, and began to wait.

Around eleven thirty, I heard movement and went to the door. The catering manager had finished a stocktake in the storeroom. He had seen the light in my office and was looking for me. He took over while I rang the emergency social worker line at the local council. The phone rang out! I sat for a moment but could see no alternative. I rang the police.

Two police officers arrived, and coaxed the young woman to leave the room and let them take her to an emergency centre.

A few days later, one of the art teachers knocked on my office door and entered.

'Warden,' he said. 'I need to explain about Melanie.'

'I'm not sure that you do,' I said. 'Unless criminal charges are likely.'

The art teacher looked appalled.

I pressed on. '…or lawsuits.'

'Dear god,' the art teacher said. 'No. No, nothing like that.'

'How is Melanie?'

'She's much better. Stephanie has been looking after her and she's going to move back in with…'

I cut him short. Using his family name rather than his first name for the first time in the three years I had been at the college, I told him I did not want to know.

Wooden birds in the south of France

Andrew Fisher and I met at Sydney University in 1959 when we were still in our (late) teens, and we remained close friends until his death in 2015. Both of us spent a good number of years living in London.

Andrew and I wrote revue sketches and film scripts together. We enjoyed the experience. This was in the pen and paper (and Olivetti portable typewriter) days, and we would throw ideas around and laugh and tear the pen out of the other's hands and take over in mid-sentence.

We got two of our scripts made into short films, but the lasting result of our scriptwriting was that we came to understand how each other thought. We could finish each other's sentences, or leave out several intermediate stages in a conversation because we knew where the other was going. When Andrew and I were conversing and getting carried away on some fantasy or other, Marianne would shake her head and wander away. Andrew died a good number of years ago now, and yet I still feel an all-enveloping sorrow when Marianne and I talk about him.

Andrew came and spent some time with Marianne and me at the house in the south of France. The first time was in 1970. He came with his then partner Val, and I remember him lying on his back next to the swimming pool and holding the five-month-old Alicia up in the air above him, and Alicia making gurgling noises of pleasure.

Andrew came to the family house a second time, in 1979. I met him and his then partner Bethany at Marignane, the airport for Marseilles, and drove them the hundred and seventy kilometres back to the house.

Andrew arrived wearing London clothes, consisting of a dark jacket and dark trousers that accentuated his tall, almost spindly figure. Our kids had called him 'Uncle Andrew' from the moment they could say the words, and they rushed to greet him when he got out of the car. They danced around him as he and Bethany came in through the garden gate. Andrew dug into his bag and gave them presents that he had bought from a specialist shop for model makers in Soho – two ingenious wooden birds that were powered by rubber bands and actually flew. The kids insisted on trying them out, and they dragged Andrew into the field beside the house.

Andrew wound the birds up and set them flying. They circled in the air, flapping chaotically, and Frank aged four, Alicia aged six, and Andrew aged forty-eight, chased after them, shouting and laughing, waving their arms in the air, and skipping and spinning in the silvery provençale sunlight.

Telling the truth in le midi

I am struck by how similar the countryside is in the south of France (le midi) and the Greek Peloponnesus. No surprise, really. Both regions seem to have the same rocks bleached grey-white by the sun, the same vegetation hugging the ground, the same cliff faces with hidden, mysterious caves… The similarities are so great that I can imagine coming across a pool of cool water in le midi and seeing Greek nymphs sunning themselves at the water's edge, and one or two of the gods, let's say Artemis and her twin Apollo, indolently floating in the water. Of course, the water would have magical properties.

It was 1980, and the kids and I were at the family house in the south of France. For some reason, neither Achille nor Marianne was there and so Mathilde asked me to drive her to a cocktail party at a friend's house some fifteen or so kilometres further into the hinterland of the Var. I did so, with Mathilde sitting in the back seat as she always did, rather than in the passenger seat next to me. As a result, conversation was difficult and all attempts at it were rapidly abandoned. I engaged in some irritated thought about how in Australia many people get into the front passenger seat of a taxi with the express purpose of chatting with the driver, and that they do this to demonstrate that theirs is a transaction between equals.

We arrived at the friend's house. It was typically provençale, thick stone walls, two storeys, the traditional blue wooden shutters on the windows, and a three-layered Roman tile roof. Beautiful. The house was halfway up a hillside and had a level terrace around it, overlooking the lines of vines stretching away on the valley floor.

The drinks were being served on the terrace, and I was out of the car and had a drink in my hand before my mother-in-law, with whom anything was possible, could suggest it might be better if I waited in the car.

The host was a charming man, with a wistful air about him. He latched on to me for some reason. He showed me around the house, and then took me a little way uphill behind the house to a natural pool, worn out of the rocks by millennia of cool, clear water flowing from a hidden spring. The water ran rapidly and the pool was deep. It was one of those small miraculous works of nature. The host appeared to be in no hurry to return to his guests, and we lingered, chatting but also standing there in silence. I knelt down, cupped my hands, and drank.

We went back down the hillside, and parted company. I wandered amiably amongst the other guests, paying not too much attention to anything, and ended up towards one end of the terrace.

Close behind me, I heard Mathilde's voice. She was talking about the family house as if it fell just short of being a nationally listed chateau. I glanced round. She was talking to a slender, elderly woman who had grey hair, was dressed in grey and had a grey pallor to her face. Both women were seated. The grey woman had a distant look in her eyes, and I learned later that she was a duchess or a countess or something else aristocratic. I turned back to look at the crowd of guests, and tuned out of their conversation, until I heard my name – Mi-koll.

'He was born in Australia,' Mathilde was saying, 'but his father is English and his mother was Irish.'

This was untrue. I had indeed been born in Australia, but so had my father, and so had his parents. My mother had been born in Australia, and so had both her parents. It was safe to say that I was an Australian of three generations, but I decided to augment the figure for effect, and so I turned and said to the grey woman, 'That is not entirely accurate, madame. In fact, I am five generations Australian, on both sides of my family.'

The ghost of a smile passed across the grey woman's pallid face, and I moved away before my mother-in-law could remonstrate in any way. How had I come to so openly contradict her? Perhaps that magic pool had affected me in some way. I had drunk deep at the spring. Well, not deep, but I had drunk. Perhaps I had thought for a moment that we could all stop the charade. Perhaps the duchess could say she was not remotely interested in my mother-in-law's house. Perhaps the host could tell the guests that they bored him, and that they should go home now. Perhaps I could refuse to drive Mathilde home unless she sat in the passenger seat next to me.

But of course I did not – the relationship was bad enough as it was – and we drove home in silence.

Fire in London

One evening, during my time as warden of the Working Men's College, I was at my desk doing some paper work. It was around nine fifteen p.m. and the outer office was closed, but my office had a second door giving on to a corridor. There was a discreet knock, and a stranger entered.

'I was passing in the street outside and I thought you should know that there's smoke pouring out of one of the windows on the top floor.'

I thanked him and went out of the building, looked up and could see he was right. There was an awful lot of smoke. I raced back in, set the alarm going, and rang 999. Most classes finished at nine p.m. but a few went on to nine thirty, and a good number of people lingered in the common room, which had a bar. There would have been twenty or thirty people still in the building. People began leaving. I went up the stairs to the art class, whose teacher had, as I suspected, said it must be a fire drill. I told them that it was not a fire drill, and to get out of the building as soon as possible.

Once I was as sure as I could be that the building was empty, I went out into the street. A grubby, down-at-heel young man was standing just outside the front doors at the top of the steps. I went to tell him to get away from the building but saw that he had a radio phone, and realised he was a plain clothes policeman.

He asked me who I was, and I told him, and he said, 'The fire chief will want to talk to you.' He pointed to a small group of firefighters who were standing in front of a huge fire truck on the other side of the street.

Other fire fighters were closing off the street, and another fire truck was arriving, sirens howling and then winding down into silence.

I reported to the fire chief. At first sight, he was an unprepossessing figure, but that impression was brief. He was held in evident respect by the firefighters around him, and when he spoke it was with a calm but compelling authority. We quickly cleared up the problem with my title of warden.

'So you're the man in charge. They spell your title with a capital W like in Oxford?'

'Something like that.'

'Can we go, guv? Can we go?' Two quite small men were standing on either side of the fire chief.

'Not just yet, lads. Let's learn something about the building first.' He looked back at me and then fired off questions: how many staircases were there, was the room the smoke was pouring out of a classroom (it was one of three small music rehearsal rooms, each with a piano in it), was there anything above it, what was below it, what level was it on (it was on the fifth level)?

'Can we go, guv? Can we go?'

'Not just yet, lads.' The fire chief was calmness personified, the two men beside him like eager puppies.

Satisfied with my answers, the fire chief looked up at the window bellowing smoke, fell silent for an agonising moment, and then nodded at the two puppies, who raced across the road, up the steps and into the building. I have rarely seen two happier people. This was what they lived for: going into dangerous places, the excitement, seeking out and reporting on the seat of fire, the first in, the ones who led the way. The reconnaissance men!

'Now,' the fire chief said to me, 'we wait.'

But not for long. The chief's radio phone crackled, incomprehensibly for me but not for him. I watched his face, and he was nodding and smiling. The crackling stopped and the chief walked over to a group of firefighters who were kitted up with breathing gear and portable extinguishers. He spoke to them briefly, then touched the leader on the arm to restrain him for a moment, and looked back at me.

'Is this music room likely to be locked?'

'No,' I said. 'No lock.'

The chief nodded at the men and they entered the building.

The chief walked back to me. 'The fire's contained to the one room,' he said. 'We can fight it from inside the building. That way we avoid water damage. I make no promises, of course.'

Time passed. Smoke stopped coming out of the window. The radio crackled.

'We can go in now.'

We walked in, up four flights of stairs and along a corridor to the three music rooms. The door of the middle room was open, the piano badly damaged, the room blackened.

The fire chief looked at me. 'Could you stand back out of the way, warden?'

I withdrew down the corridor. The chief and the team leader consulted, decided that the floor was safe and went into the room. They spent time looking and talking.

The chief came out and approached me. 'We think the fire started in the piano, but we don't know how. Of course, you can always blame a dropped cigarette, but we think that's unlikely. The soundproofing tiles kept the fire contained and stopped it going into the roof.' His words were unsettling.

'Do you think it was deliberately lit?'

He ignored my question, and said, 'Come with me, warden.' (He seemed to enjoy using my title.) 'We'll have a little wander. What's on the other side of this corridor?' He indicated the corridor we had come along.

'Two classrooms.'

We went to the first one, and he opened the door and looked in. Nothing. We opened the door to the next classroom, and looked in.

The fire chief seemed interested. He pointed to the back of the room. 'A cupboard,' he said. 'Let's have a look.'

We went into the room and walked between the tables and chairs to the back. The fire chief opened the cupboard. On a shelf at about eye level there were crumpled sheets of paper, partly blackened and still smouldering.

'Now,' the fire chief said, his voice taking on a schoolmasterly tone, 'one seat to a fire, and it can be an accident, but two seats to a fire means arson.'

We reported the fire, and the fire chief's conclusion that it was deliberately lit, to the police, but nothing came of it. For the next few evenings, I was very nervous, and the building manager and I checked the building as thoroughly as we could after everyone had gone. The majority of our classes met once a week, and so, when we came to the same day the next week, three of my colleagues and I patrolled the building throughout the evening, and did a very thorough inspection after we had locked up.

Time passed, and no more attempts on the building were made. All this happened in late 1980. I left in the middle of 1982. The five-storey Edwardian building is still there.

PS: The women's movement was in full voice during the time I was at the college, and there were regular agonised and sometimes heated debates in the college council meetings about the college name. The college had been founded in 1854 by the Christian Socialists (about whom my dad had written!) to provide 'a liberal education for members of the artisan and working classes'. Among the Christian Socialists' number were Frederick Denison Maurice, a rumblingly powerful, charismatic theologian; Tom Hughes, author of *Tom Brown's Schooldays*; Charles Kingsley, author of *The Water Babies* and several novels depicting the struggles of the working class; John Ludlow, a convinced socialist with extensive contacts with socialists in France; Frederick James Furnivall (a prominent literary scholar); and John Westlake, who was the son of a Cornish wool stapler and who held a chair in international law at Cambridge.

The first art teachers at the college were John Ruskin (one of the great English intellectuals of the Victorian era) and Dante Gabriel Rossetti (a leading light amongst the Pre-Raphaelite painters).

In the debates about the college's name, the traditionalists saw the name as a part of the college's rich history and wanted to keep it unchanged. The progressives argued vigorously that more women than men were enrolled at the college, making 'Working Men's College' a misnomer, and that in any event the name was an awful patriarchal anachronism. A compromise had been arrived at shortly before my arrival, and so I was obliged to print on the cover of the college prospectus 'The Working Men's College for Women and Men'.

A humdinger of a lowlight

In 1982, Marianne, the kids and I resettled from London to Sydney, leaving our friends, our jobs, our house, and what had been our country of residence for the past fourteen years. The wrench was huge. Marianne was in the process of consolidating a full-time job at the City Literary Institute in London's West End as a trainer of language teachers. Alicia was happy at Haverstock High School, and had a strong group of friends. Frank was at Primrose Hill Primary School. He was the goalkeeper in an under-eleven soccer team, and had a very strong friendship with two of his schoolmates.

Marianne says leaving Europe was traumatic. She acknowledges that the word is overused but maintains that in her case it is accurate. We have a photo of the four of us, taken by Andrew on the morning of our departure. Each one of us looks ill.

My mother-in-law did not talk to me, or even ask after me, for the next ten years.

We left the UK because I had been headhunted for the post of director of the Workers' Educational Association in Sydney. It sounds nice but the job was a dud. The volunteer management of the WEA was riven with factional infighting. The morale of the paid staff was poor. The finances were in disarray. The educational program lacked direction. And early on in my tenure, in a test of my strength, the president of the association overrode me and sacked one of my staff!.

I wrote to the membership, calling on them to support a vote of no confidence in the president, and battle was joined. Gradually, with the help of people inside and outside the association, I wrested control back to a point where I could re-employ the sacked member of staff, and appoint a qualified and experienced accountant. Together, the three of us set about restructuring the association's finances and rebuilding the educational program.

A year, almost to the day after I took up the job, I drove to the apartment of the newly elected president of the association. I reassured him that the organisation was in good educational and financial shape, and said, 'You've had five years' of my life in one, and that's enough.' I worked out a short period of notice and, carrying a cardboard box (yes!), I walked out of the association's offices and into unemployment.

And in the middle of all this, my dad died. I am not going to describe my grief, but I am going to describe one glorious feature of his going. Dad died while sitting at a small table in the living room of the family house. The doctor opined that he had leaned back from whatever he was doing, yawned and had a heart attack.

When the funeral people took Dad's body away, and the doctor departed, we could see what Dad had been working on at his small table. It was his income tax return.

Risking all in Wodonga

I had made some friends during my struggles at the Workers' Educational Association and, with their help, I began working as a trainer in the Trade Union Training Authority (TUTA), at first part-time, and then, in early1984, full-time.

TUTA had been set up in 1975 by the Labor federal government to provide education and training for trade unionists. I lived in Sydney but did most of my work at a residential college called Clyde Cameron College in a town called Wodonga in the north of the state of Victoria. I would take a Sunday afternoon flight from Sydney to Wodonga and conduct courses at the college that lasted one, two or three weeks. The group would meet for a preliminary session at seven thirty on Sunday evening, and the courses proper would start at eight thirty the next morning.

In early 1985, I ran a two-week course for senior workplace reps in the oil industry. There were sixteen participants, and the session on Sunday evening was short, consisting of a briefing about the course and a quick round of two- to three-minute introductions. The majority of the participants came off oil rigs, a couple of them were divers, and the rest were from refineries. Almost all of them were big, lanky blokes, amiable enough, but not people with whom I would want to have a serious disagreement. We went to the bar at about eight thirty, and dispersed to our rooms reasonably quickly after that. In the bar, I felt the participants were ready to give me the benefit of the doubt, but only for the time being.

The first morning session involved some input from me about the current industrial relations scene, a period of small-group discussion in which people could put their own views, and then a round-up in the full group again. Some fifteen minutes into the session, I could sense the participants' attention was wandering and one of them, called Jamie, spoke up.

'Listen, Mike. We work outdoors.'

'And under water,' one of the divers said.

'And we're not used to sitting still for so long.'

'We stop here,' I said. 'Get up, go out of the room, and talk among yourselves. I'm here if there's any college info you want. Come back in ten minutes, and we'll decide what to do.'

It is standard practice in adult training to hand problems back to the participants, and reduce one's own role to that of a resource, but there's always a risk. What if some silly bugger proposes conducting the rest of the course in a Wodonga pub? It was with this possibility in mind that I sent them out of the training room into the corridor. It meant that I continued to occupy the training room, and the authority implicit in that.

They were out for ten minutes and not a second more. Punctuality is important on an oil rig. They trooped back in and proposed two ten-minute breaks per session, and the odd five-minute break when the opportunity arose.

'What about the time lost?' I asked.

Jamie replied. 'We can get some of that back by going on for an extra fifteen minutes into the lunch and dinner breaks.'

We spent the last twenty minutes of this first session preparing questions to put to an official from the Australian Council of Trade Unions, who was scheduled to address them in the second session. I tracked the official down during the morning break and explained our group's decision to have ten-minute pauses.

'Bugger that,' the official said. 'I've flown up from Melbourne this morning to talk to these blokes and they are just going to have to wear it. I've got a lot to cover.'

The second session was not a success. Some of the bigger blokes began shifting uneasily and waving their arms and legs about, a bit like kids in a kindergarten. Others entered a kind of catatonic state. The divers looked serene, and one of them was rocking gently from side to side. Impervious to this, the ACTU official droned on, leaving no time at the end for the questions the group had prepared.

On our way to the cafeteria for lunch Jamie said to me, 'Why didn't you tell that silly bastard about our ten-minute breaks?'

'I did.'

'Why didn't you insist?'

'Why didn't you?' I said, and we looked at each other.

This brief conversation was illuminating. If I wanted to stop everything becoming my fault, then I would have to do something to save the situation, and do it quickly. I peeled off before we got to the cafeteria, got the keys for the college car, and drove into Wodonga. There, I found a shop that sold sweets, and I bought a packet of boiled lollies – pieces of hard candy that are wrapped in cellophane and closed with a twist at both ends. I got back to the college, grabbed and ate a banana, put the lollies loose in my pockets, and headed for the training room and the first of the two afternoon sessions.

The session was about solving problems and I had a perfect example from the morning. I kicked the session off by getting the group to discuss how they had arrived at the decision to have ten-minute breaks. 'There's a process in all this,' I said and ran a short trigger film showing a problem developing in a workplace. The film ends with a number of options but no resolution. When the film came to an end, I said, 'I'm going to ask you a series of questions, and there's a prize for whoever gives me the right answer first.'

The group looked at me.

I asked my first question, one of the participants answered, and I took a lolly out of my pocket and threw it to him. Now, this was one of those moments. Once the lolly was airborne, there was no turning back. As it flew through the air in a beautiful arc, I thought to myself, 'There goes my career.'

The participants were seated around heavy wooden desks arranged in the shape of a U. My throw was not all that accurate, and the person who answered had to jump up and lean over the desk to catch the lolly. This meant that he was standing, and he remained standing as he unwrapped the lolly slowly, and popped it into his mouth. He sat down and looked round the room with a smirk on his face.

I asked another question, and several people shouted out an answer. I threw another lolly, and the mood had changed. I tried to be even-handed in the way I threw the lollies, and most people got one, but one participant kept missing out. When he finally got a lolly, there was cheering and laughter. We had one of their breaks, and the rest of the course went well.

As the course progressed, the participants got caught up in the exercises and scenarios, and abandoned their ten-minute breaks but still worked into their lunch and dinner breaks. On the second Wednesday, when I said for the second time that they should stop for lunch and no one took any notice of me, I looked across at Jamie, and he shrugged.

Lunch with my sister-in-law in le Marais

It was important for me to maintain my residence and employment rights for the UK, in case we wanted to go back there. To do that, I had to re-enter the UK within three years, even if only for a few days. When the three years were nearly up, we decided that Marianne would stay in Sydney with the kids, and I would travel to the UK alone. I intended flying there and back, but I could not return to Europe without paying court to my parents-in-law. And so it was, as they say in the story books, that I flew into Paris one Tuesday afternoon in June 1985.

My plane touched down at Charles de Gaulle airport. I was staying at a nephew's, so took a taxi from the airport to his apartment in the eighteenth arrondissement, rested up there for an hour or two, and then made my way for dinner in an apartment I did not know in the eleventh arrondissement.

Shortly after Marianne, the kids and I had left for Australia, Laetitia and Jean-Claude separated. They had been together for nearly twenty-eight years. Laetitia took up with a new partner sixteen years her junior, and Jean-Claude took up with a new partner eleven years his junior.

Laetitia answered the door of the apartment and ushered me into the living room, and I saw that all four players were present. I greeted Jean-Claude, and was introduced to his new partner, Ditte, and then to Laetitia's new and youthful partner, Eric. A surreal conversation followed in which I answered questions about Marianne and the kids, and we chatted about my flight. The two men gave grunts betokening interest, and the two women little gasps of excitement as I spoke of uninteresting things, like my two-hour stopover in Singapore.

We assembled at the dining table. I was placed at the end, and the couples sat facing each other. Laetitia was doing the cooking, and she and Eric brought the food to the table. Laetitia's cooking was always excellent. At least I had that to look forward to. The evening progressed, with the two newly formed couples engaging in apparently light-hearted banter. At one stage, they even began discussing the kind of holiday the four of them might go on together. The evening was fast turning into a parody of French manners. I pleaded jet lag, took the metro to my nephew's apartment, and slept the sleep of the dead. I didn't dream.

I woke mid-morning, got dressed, left the apartment, and set off to meet Laetitia for lunch. After having five children, Laetitia had written a Master's thesis on Giacometti, and then landed a job at Centre Pompidou, one of the most prestigious, and most visited, museums in the world. She had risen quickly, and now was head of one of its departments. I walked into the massive lobby of the museum, and saw Laetitia on the far side, walking in my direction and giving instructions to two acolytes, one on either side of her. She had not seen me and so I could look at her and marvel. My sister-in-law, was wearing a matador hat on an extravagant angle, and a cloak flung across the shoulders of a tailored jacket (with enormous black buttons) and a swirling skirt reaching down to just above her calf-length boots. How had a kid from Queanbeyan come to be a part of all this?

At that moment, she saw me, and cried out, 'Mi-eek.' (Mike, to you and me.)

The two acolytes peeled away and were gone. Laetitia and I kissed each other on both cheeks, and headed out of the museum and into the narrow streets of one of the oldest parts of Paris, known as le Marais. Laetitia led me to a small bistro, where her secretary had booked a table for us, and we sat down.

As in most Parisian restaurants that do lunch, the tables were small and close together. If there is more than a five-centimetre gap between the tables, then they are considered separate. The people at the table next to you may be almost touching you and you may be able to hear every word they say, but the convention is that you ignore them, and they ignore you.

Laetitia and I ordered, and waited until our wine was served. We then saluted each other by touching our glasses and sipping the wine. Once this had been done, we could talk.

'Tell me, Mi-eek, what do you think of my little act of madness, *ma petite folie?*' This conversation took place in French.

'What madness is that?'

'The separation. My lover.'

There was a woman at the next table. Her shoulder was practically rubbing mine. She was holding a book in her left hand, and toying with her food with a fork in her right hand. She put her fork down, turned the page of her book with a discreet flicking sound, and picked up her fork again.

'Well, I hate the idea that you and Jean Claude have split up, but I like your new partner. '

'He's clever, and very witty. Did you enjoy the evening?'

'To be frank, no,' I said, and went on in my clumsy French. 'I didn't know what the four of you were playing at. You were showing off. I felt like I was in some second-rate play.'

I had felt a sudden rush of anger, and I had spoken a little more loudly. The woman next to me put down her fork, turned over the page of her book, and picked her fork up again. Laetitia sat there in silence. Here was a woman I had known and admired for more than twenty years, and I had just hurt her.

I tried to repair the damage. 'Look, Laetitia, it just seemed so artificial. What were you all doing together? If you and Jean-Claude really have split up, then why aren't you and your new lover off in the mountains, making love passionately?'

The woman next to me turned the page of her book. It seemed a very short time since she had turned the last one.

There was a moment of cross-cultural miscommunication. Laetitia seemed to think I was doubting the passion of her new lover because she said, 'You know, Mi-eek, I may be older than him but he loves playing with my body. He loves…'

The woman next to me turned the page of her book with a loud slapping noise, and Laetitia and I moved on to less anatomical subjects.

When we were parting at the end of our lunch, any anger of mine forgiven, Laetitia told me that her parents, aka my parents-in-law, did not know that she and Jean-Claude had split up, and under no circumstances was I to tell them. I did not like being committed to a lie, but she made me promise.

I spent the evening with two nephews and their partners in a down-at-heel Moroccan restaurant in the twentieth arrondissement. I had not met the partner of the younger of the nephews before. She is a Scot, and we clicked immediately. She married into the family a few months later, and, in the richest of Aberdeen accents, calls Marianne 'Aunty Mary'.

I was flying on to London late the next afternoon and still had the most important duty to perform, and that was to lunch with my parents-in-law. I turned up at their apartment with my bag, and was let in by my father-in-law. My mother-in-law appeared briefly, in a dressing gown hanging open and with her hair all awry, and explained that she had a high fever and would go back to bed. I was to lunch with my father-in-law and he would tell her all about it later. I wondered about her fever. In the normal course of events, Mathilde and I would have given each other the lightest of kisses on both cheeks, but she had been furious with me (hated me might be more accurate) for taking her daughter to Australia, and I suspected the fever was a ruse to avoid touching my detestable person at all.

Achille and I repaired to the living room, sat at a table near the window and ate the lunch that was already laid out there. After the second glass of wine, and with the lunch finished, my father-in-law asked me who I had seen since I arrived in Paris. I said I had seen Laetitia and Jean-Claude, and two of his grandsons. He asked me if I had noticed any changes in Laetitia. I said, no, I had not. He looked at me, and I looked unblinkingly back.

After a while, Achille looked away and stared out the window. I should be on my way, he said. I asked him to say goodbye to Mathilde for me, took my bag and made my way to Charles de Gaulle airport by the fast underground train known by the initials RER. Just you try pronouncing that in French.

Laetitia should never have asked me to lie to my parents-in-law, but she did and I opted to be guided by generational loyalty. From the way Achille looked at me, I knew he knew I was lying. But he said nothing. Perhaps, like me, he did not want to upset the apple cart. Families can be delicate affairs.

Brothers-in-law in Paris

Jean-Claude had married Marianne's sister Laetitia in 1954, fourteen years before I entered the French family. They separated in 1983, but did not get divorced until just before Jean-Claude's death in 1990, which meant that he and I were brothers-in-law for fifteen or twenty-three years, depending on how you look at things.

Jean-Claude was a graduate of École Normale Superieure, one of a group of *grandes écoles* (literal translation: big schools), which are the training grounds for the French elite. Entry is by competition. Applying requires several years of preparation. And then, only a minimal number, no more than five per cent of the applicants, get accepted.

Graduating from a *grande école* marked Jean-Claude out as super-bright and super-promising, and all but guaranteed him lifetime employment in the upper echelons of the French public service. The education he received was of the highest standard and he graduated knowing just about everything about everything – or at least, that is the impression he gave. All this made him a little pompous. In discussions, he could become intransigent and adopt the tone of a teacher whose duty was to instruct those around him.

Jean-Claude and I developed an affectionate relationship. He had made an early move. It was on Marianne's and my wedding day, at the reception in the afternoon. Jean-Claude approached me and addressed me in English.

He spoke very carefully, holding up his right hand with the tip of his index finger touching the tip of his thumb, and gesturing to emphasise each syllable, 'Mi-eek, now you are my broth-er.'

It was nearing the end of a long day, in which my very limited French had been sorely tested. I looked at him and replied in English,

'And you are mine.'

Two months after our wedding, Marianne and I were in Paris, and attending a family lunch at the apartment of my parents-in-law. Laetitia, Jean-Claude and their children arrived. Jean-Claude was looking grim, and after the briefest of greetings he went out on to the balcony. There, I could see him gulping in air and fighting for control. I waited a while, and then joined him, and we looked in silence down at the street five storeys below, and up at the Eiffel Tower, which was just a few streets away. As I came to understand, Jean-Claude, the apparent superman, could pass through periods of crippling self-doubt.

Mathilde and Achille bought the house in the south in late 1968, and the family gathered there for the first time in the summer of 1969. On the first morning, I went into the garden. Jean-Claude was sitting there reading. I sat down with him, and he opened the conversation by asking me what kind of influence Nietzsche had on my thinking. Of course, philosophy is taught from quite early on in French high schools, but even so.

'Ah, Nietzsche,' I said in what was, I hoped, a mysterious way, and I got up and wandered away in a mild panic. Would Jean-Claude be in the garden every morning, lying in wait for me? Would he want my views tomorrow morning on Heidegger? Was there a way of getting to the swimming pool by not passing through the garden? I could be sick, of course, but not for the whole summer.

I had misjudged my new brother. He realised he had embarrassed me, and did not do it again. But there was no denying that we differed radically one from the other. I had brought a good supply of books in English, and read through them in groups of three. One would be a respectable book, like a Dickens or something by Lawrence Durrell, the next would be a good quality thriller, and the third would be holiday pulp. My intention was to amuse myself. Jean-Claude brought with him books by Goethe, or Dante, or Heraclitus (yes), or other tracts of an intellectually challenging nature. His intention was, I suppose, to improve himself.

The difference was also evident at the swimming pool. Jean-Claude would do exercises, serious ones like push-ups, which he would do with a terrible intensity in multiples of twenty. And he would do them in the sun, so that his body became the colour of a walnut. I hid in the shade of a beach umbrella so that my wretched Anglo-Celtic skin stayed white, reading or just anticipating the pleasures of the next meal. And Jean-Claude wore tiny little speedos just one degree short of being a cache-sex, while I wore baggy swimming trunks, which seemed to catch the air and billow out when I entered the water.

Every now and again, I would play the clown, and Jean-Claude would laugh, not his usual minimal number of woeful barking sounds, but a large, open, generous laugh. When that happened, we would grin at each other, which I took as his way of saying thank you.

In 1989, I attended a conference in the UK, and stopped over in Paris to pay court to Mathilde and Achille. During a family dinner, I realised that I was missing Jean Claude, and I rang him the next morning. Look, I said, just because he had withdrawn from the family did not mean that he and I had to lose contact with each other. He invited me to his apartment in Pigalle, where we had an amicable lunch. The affection was still there, and it was late in the afternoon when he accompanied me to the metro, and we said our goodbyes.

I should have thought a little before I spoke, but at the top of the steps leading down into the metro I stopped and said the utterly conventional thing, in French, 'You should come to Australia.'

Jean-Claude considered my words, and then said, 'What for? *Pourqoi faire?*'

What for? What for? Pourquoi bloody faire? Because I love you, you silly bastard, I thought as I waited on the platform for the next train.

Jean-Claude began losing weight at an alarming rate in late 1989, and in early 1990 was diagnosed with a galloping lung cancer. He died two months later. Jean-Claude's partner Ditte, Laetitia and her partner Eric, and all the five children and their partners rallied around in those last weeks. Marianne and I stayed in touch by phone.

A few days before the end, I spoke to Jean-Claude. 'Do you remember,' I said to him, 'how you came up to me at Marianne's and my wedding reception and said to me that we were now brothers?'

'And we still are,' he said, and then in English, 'Broth-ers.'

I imagined him holding up his hand with the tip of the index finger touching the tip of his thumb, and emphasising each syllable with a slight gesture. Typical of the man, he left behind him a scholarly work on Heraclitus (yes, again), on which he had worked until quite close to the end.

Pourquoi faire: was it insulting or not? Marianne and I have talked this over and come up with three possible explanations. The first lies in the simple fact that the French can be blunt. In English, we soften requests with phrases like 'Would you mind...' or 'If it's no trouble, could you...' French does not seem to have these kinds of phrase. An everyday request, like 'Close the door. *Tu ferme la porte*' will have no please in it, and the person being addressed doesn't expect there to be one. Jean-Claude may have been inept, but he was not being insulting. He was asking a question. In French.

The second reason is not so straightforward. Marianne and I have encountered something of the same attitude in two close friends of ours.

One, Patrick, has only rarely travelled outside France and he makes it quite clear that it is by choice. France, he has told us more than once, has everything you could want within its borders: towering mountains, the rugged coastline of Brittany, the farmlands of Normandy, the beaches of the Riviera, the hill villages in Provence, the food and wine, forests, rivers and canals, chateaux, cathedrals, churches, and some of the finest museums in the world.

The other friend, Bruno Bontempelli, now sadly gone, was an established novelist, and he had a passion for the French language that obliterated any interest in other languages or the countries that went with them. No, the French language was unique, beautiful, something far superior to the untidiness of English or the order of German, or the indiscipline of the other latin languages.

Which leads us to the tentative conclusion that Jean-Claude's *pourquoi faire* may have been inept, but it was not an expression of arrogance. It was a statement made by a man comfortable in his own culture, a condition that those of us from new, less established cultures may not have experienced.

And our third explanation is to do with how we come to understand each other. In Anglophone contexts, we tend to ask people where they come from and what they do. Some French people display no interest in such details. When Jean-Claude mentioned Nietzsche, he may have frightened me, but he wanted to talk about ideas. He wanted to understand who I was by understanding how I thought.

At the top of the steps down to the metro, Jean-Claude paused and thought about my invitation before saying '*Pourquoi faire*'. Yes, he was being socially inept, but perhaps he was saying that he did not need to go to Australia. After years as in-laws in the same family, and sharing that oddly insider-outsider status, each of us already had a good idea of how the other one thought.

On love, on love

In 1985, I was asked to coordinate a two-day course for twenty-two job representatives (shop stewards) of the Metropolitan Water and Sewerage Employees' Union. The MWSEU covered people who kept the water and sewage of Sydney moving. I worked on the course along with the secretary of the union, and the union's research officer, and we covered the union's history, a little about the industrial relations system in general, a lot about the particular agreement covering their members, and the key union skills of representing a member, negotiation, and managing a meeting.

The secretary was Joe Fisher, a no-nonsense man who opened his section on the union's history with the words, 'I won't take long because I don't know much.'

There had been a hiccup when we were planning the course. When Joe was outlining what he wanted the troops to learn, he made particular mention of formal meeting procedure.

'Why formal meeting procedure?' I said. 'Surely, when a job rep calls a meeting at a plant or a depot, they discuss the problem and arrive at a consensus. Wouldn't it be better if I looked at the way informal groups work?'

Joe looked at me for a while, and then said, 'I want you to do formal meeting procedure.' He had a gravelly voice.

I said, 'Right.'

The reps were a cheerful lot. There was a lot of banter, both before we started and once the course was underway. But it was more than just good humour. It was companionship. Working metres underground had a levelling effect. And trust. Working in a potentially dangerous job meant they had to look after each other.

The tone was set the moment Joe began introducing me. One of the participants interrupted him. The matter raised had nothing to do with Joe's introduction, but nobody seemed to mind. Joe dealt with the interruption, finished up, and I began the first session.

I was accepted genially enough but certainly not with a respectful silence. Participants felt free to interject, offer me advice, and weigh up what I was saying against their own experience. It was clear that this was their course, not the secretary's, and not mine.

There were people who stood out. There was a large man in his late fifties, articulate, completely bald, no eyebrows, clad in black and wearing tall black leather boots. There was a young man, younger than most, who was unremarkable in appearance but whose opinion was regularly sought.

'What do you make of that, Nick?'

I was handing out printed instructions for an exercise and one of the participants said, 'You're wasting your time giving me one of those, Mike. I can't read.'

And there was a dark-haired, dark-eyed man who sat silent, watching me attentively throughout the two days, but who did not say a word during any of the sessions.

'Are you having trouble understanding my English?' I asked him during a break.

'No,' he replied.

We came to the last session of the course: my session on formal meeting procedure. I used a film as the starting point for talking about the elements of a meeting and the factors we need to bear in mind to control those elements. The session went smoothly, with unsolicited comments at a level I had come to accept as normal. Finally, with about forty-five minutes to go, we began an exercise in which we would work stage by stage through the process of putting a motion to a meeting, seconding it, debating it, amending it and voting on it.

'Let's assume that we have a motion that says, "This meeting of members of the MWSEU condemns management for moving the time clock from the gates to the workshop doors and calls upon its –"'

'They wouldn't do that, Mike.'

'Wouldn't do what?'

'Move the clock.'

'Not on our site.'

'Look, that doesn't matter. I'm just giving it as an example.' The example is a hoary one. If the clock is at the gates, you walk to work on the boss's time. If it's at the workshop door, you walk to work on your own time.

'His example's no good.'

'Give him a go.'

'What's the point if it'd never happen?'

The debate continued on three levels: whether or not my choice of example was appropriate; whether or not the union would brook such behaviour by management; and whether I should be given a chance to continue the session.

I sat down for a while and waited until the matter was decided – by consensus, I might note. The decision went my way, I was invited to continue, and they let me take them through the stages of voting on a motion with their usual good humour.

Onwards to 2020, and I am a member of a group of six, all of us retired, who lunch together and talk politics. One of our number was bemoaning the fact that all the recent grand theories – the enlightenment, capitalism, communism, socialism, postmodernism, neo-liberalism – had failed us, and he issued the challenge to our group to come up with a new grand theory. Nothing like thinking big!

For the fun of it, I had a go, and produced a paper. In it, I said that a new kind of society would encourage love, and I used this quote from the social theorist Zygmunt Bauman:

> To love means to value the other for its otherness, to wish to reinforce its otherness, to protect the otherness and make it bloom and thrive, and to be ready to sacrifice one's own comfort, including one's own mortal existence, if that is what is needed to fulfil that intention.

Bauman's love is the polar opposite of possession. It is not mawkish. It is tough, and, if needs be, demanding.

Having quoted Bauman, I went trawling through my memory for an example of his kind of love. A number of couples came to mind, and some parents and their children, and then I recalled the riotous gang from the Metropolitan Water and Sewerage Employees' Union. Fairness, honesty, solidarity, openness, respect for each other and, yes, I think there was love.

1990s

The great disappearing act on Oxford Street, Sydney

I had a friend called Brian. We knew each other in the 1960s in London and made contact with each other again in Sydney in the 1980s. By then, he had established a chain of frock shops that sold a wide range of women's clothing, including a line of elegant underwear designed by Brian himself. I always found this fact splendidly at odds with his appearance and demeanour. Brian was a large man (not fat) and he would stand a little too close to you for comfort, lean his head to one side and forward, and stare menacingly into your eyes. His hair was often awry.

I had always thought that if I needed to talk to a neighbour who was playing loud music late into the night, I would ask Brian to accompany me and simply stand there.

Brian's largest shop was in Oxford Street, Paddington, Sydney, close to where Marianne and I lived, and he was there most Saturdays. I would stand at the entrance to the shop until I caught his eye, and he would join me and we would talk, sometimes for half an hour or longer, until, without any preliminaries beyond a nod, he would stride back into the shop.

Brian read poetry, and I came upon him leaning against the window of his shop, muttering to himself.

'Are you all right?' I asked.

'They are all so young,' he said, and began quoting from T.S. Eliot's 'The love song of J. Alfred Prufrock':

> I grow old… I grow old…
> I shall wear the bottoms of my trousers rolled.
>
> Shall I part my hair behind? Do I dare to eat a peach?
> I shall wear white-flannel trousers, and walk upon the beach.

I have heard the mermaids singing, each to each.
I do not think that they will sing to me.

'Not sure I like any of that,' I said. 'Too close to the bone.'

'You're going to have to get used to it, mate,' he said, and leant in towards me. 'Young women do not see men our age. They don't just ignore us. They don't see us.'

I protested a bit and he grew impatient.

'We do not exist,' he said. 'I'll prove it to you.' And he told me to stand beside him in the middle of the crowded pavement.

Men walking along the pavement looked at us irritably because we were blocking their path. Young children looked up at us, saw the expression on Brian's face, and scampered away. Women our own age smiled at us and we stood aside. Young women, however, peeled away at the last moment, finding a way around us without acknowledging us or giving any indication that they knew we were there.

'All right, all right,' I said. 'It's these bloody phones.'

'No, it's not. Why would the mermaids bother singing to a couple of silly old farts like you and me?'

'Speak for yourself,' I said and, without any preliminaries beyond the slightest of nods, I walked away.

Marianne and I were away in France for four months, and on the first Saturday after we got back, I strolled to Brian's shop, looking forward to seeing him. But the shop was no longer there. In its place was a sushi bar. I went in and asked for the manager, and a charming-looking woman approached me. I asked her if she had a forwarding address for Brian, but we got stuck on the meaning of the words 'forwarding address' and did not make too much progress after that. I tried to remember whether I had told Brian that I would be away. Probably not. And for commercial reasons, Brian would not have been able to tell me he was selling his business and moving on. I searched the White Pages and got two likely phone numbers, but they had been disconnected. I gave up my search quickly. We had, each in our own way, disappeared.

Bringing the state of Victoria to a halt

I imagine most of us would admit to getting a thrill when we find ourselves in the presence of greatness. In my case, greatness came in the form of a quietly spoken union official.

In mid-1986, another trainer and I ran a two-week course at Clyde Cameron College for eighteen newly elected union secretaries and presidents. They were former union activists who now found themselves responsible for budgets in the millions of dollars, the maintenance of valuable property, the management of staff, and the welfare of thousands of members. My co-trainer and I had run the course before, and I found it a buzz. The participants were eager to learn, from each other as much as from the trainers, and that meant we could run sessions with lots of interaction, and make use of a complex scenario.

We started the course on Sunday evening by giving participants three minutes each to introduce themselves. One participant stood out. His name was Larry and he was secretary of a transport workers union in the state of Victoria. His introduction was succinct, and with just enough information to leave you wanting more.

Because the participants were all busy people, I had a little speech, which I gave after the introductions. 'I know you have loads to do back at your union headquarters,' I would say, 'and that there are people who will want your advice or want you to make a decision for them. This course involves a lot of hard work and you have to throw yourselves into it, so for the next two weeks I want you to try to forget about the world outside. And please, please, please, don't ring your office.' This was in the pre-mobile phone era, but the lure of the public phones in the college foyer was irresistible for some.

For the first three days of the course, my co-trainer and I led sessions on different kinds of leader, team building, managing finances, and analysing and solving problems. On the Thursday afternoon, we set up the scenario. This involved dividing the participants into two groups, and giving them the job of preparing for the amalgamation of two unions, each of which had its different history, culture, finances, structure, constitution and rules. By Friday, we had the scenario up and running. There were no classes on Saturday but I saw both groups hard at work in the college library.

Late on the second Monday, Larry approached me. 'I have to go back to Melbourne,' he said. 'And I won't be back till Wednesday morning.'

'Hang on,' I said. 'Don't you remember what I said at the beginning of the course?'

'I know, I know. But it can't be helped. I have to go.'

'Why?'

'I can't really say.'

'Great. I can't stop you going, but it gives me the shits.'

Larry left, and I wandered off to the Monday evening session in a foul mood.

During the break between sessions on Tuesday morning, we heard that the state of Victoria was coming to a standstill. The trains were not running. At the lunch break, we crowded into the common room, where there was a television set, and watched the news. The union, we were told, had been in negotiations with management for some weeks now. This morning, its leaders had delivered an ultimatum. Management had turned them down, and the union had called a stoppage in response. Management was caught off guard because they had not believed that the union could act so quickly. Behind the newsreader were shots of empty rail lines. And then, introduced as the 'union boss' who had called the strike, Larry came on, and the course participants shouted and whistled and cheered, and I could not hear what he said. An agreement was reached and trains were running again late that afternoon. Things were approaching normal the next morning.

I went into the training room the next morning a few minutes before nine a.m., and Larry was sitting there. He smiled.

The scenario culminated with two role plays on the second Thursday. Each group played a committee of union officials meeting with their members to outline how the amalgamation would be managed and the form the new union would take. After their presentation, each group took questions, and the rest of the course participants tested and challenged everything they had said.

The two role plays took up the whole day. We held mini-debriefings after each one, then a major debriefing of both the scenario and the whole course on the Friday morning. The course ended just before lunch.

Following his return on the Wednesday morning, Larry had knuckled down and participated in the rest of the course. Now I watched him in the second role play. Others of his group did the presentation, and took questions. Larry remained silent. However, I did notice that, when a curly question was asked, the others in the group glanced his way, and he nodded at the person he thought should give the answer.

How do I describe greatness? It's a difficult question, so let me go one degree simpler and describe a great person. Then you can decide whether Larry fitted the bill. A great person provides a role model, has presence, is a mover and shaker, always acts with the general good in mind, and has an effect on history.

Grind and the silver cowboy in Texas

I visited North America for the first time in 1993. I attended the annual conference of the American Association of Adult Education, which was being held in an enormous hotel and conference centre in Dallas, Texas. Two events in the conference mystified me.

The first took place at the opening session of the conference. I found a seat about midway down the gigantic auditorium and, along with hundreds of other people, sat through the opening remarks and then a panel of experts.

When that finished, the master of ceremonies stepped up to the microphone and, adopting another accent altogether, said, 'Now the next session is the exhi-hibition, and that is in the exhi-hibition hall, and so we need someone who knows his way around Dallas to lead us all to the exhi-hibition.'

People at the back of the auditorium were laughing, and a huge voice boomed out, 'Ah know mah way round Dallas, and Ah kin show you folks the way to the exhi-hibition.'

I turned in my seat, and found myself looking down the hall at a giant dressed in an all-silver cowboy outfit. As the giant walked forward, people began laughing and applauding. The person sitting next to me explained that the giant silver cowboy was a name I have forgotten, who played in a position I did not understand in the Dallas Cowboys, the local but apparently nationally renowned American football team.

'Jess you follow me,' the giant silver cowboy roared, and as one the auditorium stood and filed after him as he sashayed through the doors, along to the left, and into the gigantic exhibition hall, where a large number of publishers and manufacturers of educational equipment had their stalls. We had gone from earnest discourse to the inanities of the sandpit, to rampant free market capitalism, all in less than five minutes.

The second mystifying event took place the following evening at a reception with nibbles and drinks provided by a major educational publisher. I got there half an hour or so late, and walked through the swinging doors into a massive space, with a stage set against a wall and a dance floor in front of the stage. High school students, dressed in red and white cowboy and cowgirl outfits, were line dancing. They were still kids and looked charming as they went through their paces.

The doors I came through were to the side of the dance floor. The kids were dancing facing the crowd, but as I came further into the room, they turned so that they faced me, and the girls suddenly held their hips, thrust their pelvises forward, and did what looked to me like a provocative grind taken from a handbook for strippers. I took a glass of anything from a passing tray. Perhaps, I told myself, the shift from wholesome to sleazy was all in my mind, and that young people of good family in Texas did the pelvic grind all the time in shopping malls, Methodist churches, swimming pools, and other public places.

As the dancers were finishing up, a voice over the sound system informed us that the dancing had been 'pro-fessio-nally ko-re-ographed'.

Getting it wrong in Dallas

I was at that conference in Dallas in 1993 to receive a prize for a book I had written. No one sought me out, and people responsible for the conference seemed difficult to find. When I did find one, she turned out to be working for a company that managed conferences on anything – adult and continuing education this week, the North American Association of Chiropractors the next – and had no knowledge of the minutiae of this particular conference, beyond the titles of the sessions printed in the conference program. But she did help, in that I looked long and hard at the printed program again and found that it did say that an awards lunch would be held on the second day. I checked the bag of papers I had been given at registration and found a ticket for the lunch, which meant that I was not cheating when I took my place at the appointed time at one of the many round tables seating ten people each.

I was wearing a jacket.

There was a rostrum with a table and a lectern on it, and a woman was on the point of assuming her place at the table.

I got up and went to her and asked her whether I was in the right place. I named the award and she said, 'Yes.'

'Do I have to make a speech?'

'I'm not sure,' she said helpfully. I resolved to watch the recipients of other awards, and do whatever they did. I went back to my place and jotted down some thoughts on a sheet of paper just in case.

A flood of waiters swept into the room, and lunch was served. Between courses the woman on the rostrum introduced two men. One of them began speaking, and after a moment or two, I realised he was glancing in my direction and talking about my book. As he went on, I learned that he was the chair of the panel that had given me the award, and that the other man was the president of the American Association of Adult Education. The chair of the panel finished and invited me to come up onto the rostrum and receive my award from the president.

I walked up the steps on to the rostrum and was given a plaque (pronounced 'plak' in American).

Both men shook my hand and said, 'Congratulations, Dr Newman.' (Pronounced Nooman in American).

'I don't have a doctorate,' I said quietly, just to them.

'Very good, Dr Nooman,' one of them said.

The two men looked at me expectantly, and the chair of the panel indicated the lectern. So I was expected to say something. I moved to the lectern and looked round the room. The woman on the rostrum looked grim, and the people around the tables seemed equally grim. I had worked as a professional actor, and I was now a university lecturer, so I had some experience in public speaking. 'In the spirit of the grind and the silver cowboy,' I thought to myself, 'I shall cheer these people up.'

I leaned close in to the mike and said, 'You know, I have a recurring dream, and it is that I am invited to speak, and as I approach the mike, I put my hand into my jacket pocket for my carefully prepared spontaneous remarks...' I paused for the laughter but there was none. (There always is in Australia, even if it's just a supportive titter.) '... but my notes are not there!'

My audience remained silent.

I ploughed on, putting my hand in my inside pocket, wiggling my fingers about as if searching for a piece of paper, and looking down at my pocket in mock distress. My audience remained silent. I lifted my notes out of my pocket, held them up and said, 'But here they are.'

My audience remained silent.

All right, that had bombed badly. Another option was to get some audience participation. I went on, 'Look, back home in a situation like this, I would be expected to give a short peroration, but I have not received any briefing for this event...' I was now having an out of body experience, and the me standing next to me told me that I had just insulted the conference organisers. 'So I am going to ask you the audience to tell me, yes or no, do I or do I not give a short and slightly pompous peroration. The me beside me was saying, 'What are you doing? Get off! Get off!'

'Can I hear the yesses?' I asked.

Absolute silence.

'And the nos?' I asked.

Absolute silence.

'No?' I said wildly. 'Then I shall have to ask madam chair next to me.' I turned to the woman seated alone at the table on the rostrum. She was looking up at me with her mouth hanging open. No help there.

I may not have actually said, 'But seriously, folks,' but I did say something along those lines, and I spoke for a minute or two, me watching me with a mixture of pity and contempt.

I went back to my table, amidst a very paltry amount of applause. I tried the starter but it turned to ashes in my mouth. I looked around the table, and realised it was an alcohol-free event!

Everyone who came after me opened with words like 'President of the association, Madam Chair, and fellow members of the association' and all of them talked of 'the great honour' the association had bestowed upon them. I had said nothing of the sort. And I noticed that if they were going to tell a joke, they told the audience they were going to tell a joke, as in 'Colleagues, I will now tell a joke.'

Of course, these sociocultural observations would be of no practical use because I was never going back to the United States of America. Never. Ever. Again. Public humiliation is a terrible thing. What if I met someone on Fifth Avenue or the beachfront at Santa Monica who had been at that lunch?

A tempest in New York

Once my Dallas disaster was over, I travelled on to New York to spend some time with Alicia. She had just completed her masters degree in theatre direction at New York University and was getting occasional gigs as an actor or assistant director, and otherwise eking out a living in the off-Broadway black economy.

I am not sure about New York. For the first few days, I found the place exciting. Being there had a vividness to it. The preposterous nature of the place made me think. But after a few days, I wanted to leave. All those things people say about New York crowded in on me: the size, the sirens, the pace and, for a Sydneysider like me, the oppressive straightness of the streets. Fifth Avenue is ten kilometres long, and straight. The road that passed through the Sydney suburb where Marianne and I lived for thirty-five years twists and turns and follows the path of the original bullock track of the early 1800s.

Alicia was in rehearsal and not free during the daytime so, after having completed my professional visits, I was left with a couple of days on my own. I was already growing edgy. I had visited museums and galleries (hours in the Whitney) but now went looking for a theatre matinee to attend, as much to get out of the crowds and into an enclosed and comfortable space as to see a play.

I wandered the streets around Times Square looking at the theatres and the billboards carrying excerpts of reviews and found a theatre where *The Tempest* was playing, with Patrick Stewart in the role of Prospero. I had seen Stewart play the part of Captain Jean-Luc Picard in the TV series *Star Trek: The Next Generation*, and was fascinated by the idea of casting him as one of Shakespeare's most complex, and powerful, characters. I bought a ticket and went to see the play.

The production was full of shifts of pace, garish, loud, wistful and subtle. All the performances were first-rate but the two movers and shakers – Prospero and his servant-spirit Ariel – were peerless. Ariel was played by a woman called Aunjanue Ellis and her performance was a combination of mystery, rebelliousness, joy and, in the magical banquet scene, staggering ferocity. Stewart gave a dynamic performance (no aged figure clutching a staff), constructing his character around the warring emotions of a love for the people and spirits on his island, and a terrible, smouldering anger.

There is a pivotal moment in the play when Ariel asks Prospero, 'Do you love me, master?' In this production, a sullen Ariel walks away, spins on her heel and, in a mercurial shift of mood, fires the question across the width of the stage. Prospero, committed to releasing Ariel when she has completed her tasks, stares back in rage, and anguish. Master and spirit. Love and anger. Father and daughter. New York had performed its magic.

Forgetting Dallas

Two years later, I found myself bound for the USA again. I had written another book and it had won the same prize as last time. This time, the conference was in Kansas City (which is in Missouri, not Kansas). Along with the letter telling me to turn up, there was a briefing. The ceremony would be held in the hotel bar at the cocktail hour. Award recipients were to speak, but for no longer than three minutes. Good, I thought, I shall say thank you, and that I am honoured, and then quit the stage and melt into air, into thin air.

Dallas had not been all bad. I had taken up with some other foreigners, none of whom, thank god, had been at the awards lunch. They were a Russian woman, a Canadian woman and two Dutchmen, and they were all back for Kansas City. We added a German man and a South Korean woman to our number, and all seven of us assembled at the cocktail hour. I was called up onto a low platform to one side of the room, and given my 'plak'. My friends were at the back of the audience, and they held their glasses high as a sign of support as I moved to the mike.

'I am honoured to receive this award,' I said, 'and I would like to thank the award committee and the association.' I stood there.

My mob at the back waved, urging me to say something else. Well, I had two minutes and fifty-five seconds left, and the temptation was too much.

'You know,' I said, 'writing is a funny business. It can take control of you. I can sit down to write, and look at my watch and it's already one o'clock in the morning. I will intend stopping after the next sentence and a moment later it is somehow half past two. And at that time of the morning I can look at what I have written and think to myself,

"Is this mad?" and then, "Am I mad?" That happened to me with this book. I was writing the final chapter and I found myself in a dialogue with my father.'

Any clinking of glasses stopped.

'He was a pacifist during the Second World War. I wanted to end my book with some kind of answer to the question of how community activists respond to violence. Does pacifism work? Do we resist passively or actively? Where's the line for active resistance? Would it ever be legitimate to initiate violence?'

I paused. Silence.

'My father died some years ago,' I said, 'and there I was in that uncanny calm between three and five in the morning, interrogating his views, challenging him, asking him for his advice…conversing with him, if you will.'

How had I got here? I thought. Why, for god's sake, was I talking about my dad to a room full of strangers?

'Thank you,' I said again, and stepped down and walked through the crowd to my friends at the back. They welcomed me and stood around me protectively. People were clapping. I was surprised by the reaction.

One of the Dutchmen, Wilhelm, was smiling broadly. 'You talked about your dead father,' he said, 'and the Americans are always touched if you talk about your family.'

As if on cue, a tall woman dressed in a classic black cocktail dress – you know, one of those ones with no back – broke through the group surrounding me. I had never seen her before. She walked up to me and enveloped me in a tight hug. She held on to me while my foreign mates looked on, then released me, looked at me for a moment with tears in her eyes, and walked away.

I could forget Dallas now.

On a clothing workers' strike in Johannesburg

I have visited South Africa three times. My first visit was in 1981. I had published a book, and I was invited to give the closing address at a conference in Durban. For some thirty years, South Africa had had a policy of apartheid, and the policy was still in place. Instead of aiming to bring about a unified nation, the policy kept the races apart. The four million whites had a vote and for them there was the semblance of a democracy. The forty million blacks and other races did not have the vote, and for them South Africa was a repressive police state.

I was living in London at the time. People were boycotting South African produce, and discouraging professional interaction with South African organisations. But the conference organisers assured me that there would be both black and white people at the conference, and that I was free to say whatever I wanted to say. I went.

It was a busy time in my London job and, ridiculous as it seems now, I flew into South Africa, delivered my paper and flew out again five days later.

I visited South Africa again in 1996, this time for seven weeks. It was six years after Nelson Mandela had walked free from prison, and two years after he was elected president. I spent time in Johannesburg, Durban and Cape Town. I went to a poetry reading in Durban. There were eighty or so people there, and lots of enthusiasm. There were poems in English and Zulu and Xhosa. The Xhosa poem was full of those clicks, and the poet made hilarious use of them in his reading. I saw blacks and whites giving each other hugs after their readings. A gathering like that a few years earlier would have been unthinkable.

There were disturbing rates of crime in the new South Africa, but there was also forgiveness and a sense of goodwill. It was a country suffused with hope. Everything seemed new. Even the most banal thing like going to the supermarket was a new experience, because the people working the checkout were black and white.

I spent ten days in Johannesburg, most of that time with the Congress of South African Trade Unions (COSATU), courtesy of an elected official, Bandile, whom I had met in Australia the year before. I did not do very much for my hosts. I contributed to a couple of courses for union representatives, was asked for advice by one or two people, and ran a seminar one evening on learning as a political tool. In return, I was welcomed and treated as an old friend by Bandile, introduced to people with stories to tell of the struggle against the apartheid regime, and taken around the picket lines of a clothing workers' strike.

Eighty thousand women across the country had been on strike for more than a week, demanding a significant wage increase across the board. The numbers on the picket lines at the Jo'burg factories seemed huge, and I was told that very few people treated the strike as time off. Virtually all the workers came into their workplaces for a full day on the picket line, travelling the long distances from the townships by minibus, bus and train, exactly as they would on a normal working day. Instead of their work clothes, they dressed for the strike in their Sunday best – berets, hats, jackets, pleated skirts – and they spent the day *toyi-toying*.

Toyi-toying is a form of communal dance accompanied by song. People, often large numbers of people, pack together and move in perfect unison, taking small steps to one side and then to the other. And they sing. This is South Africa and their singing is filled with rich, close harmonies. *Toyi-toying* can be a celebration, or it can be a form of demonstration and resistance. A mass of people singing, stamping and moving forward in unison can be an exhilarating, challenging sight.

I went round with a union organiser. She would stop her car as close as she could to the factory gates, get out, slam the car door loudly, raise both arms and begin jogging towards the crowd. The women on the picket line would come together, pick up the rhythm, begin moving in unison, and burst into song. These women were on meagre pay, and giving that up to strike meant more hardship, yet there they were in the new South Africa, solid, and determined to put the sometimes miserable conditions in which they worked to rights.

At the first picket line, the organiser was out of the car before I could say anything, and I sat there wondering what I should do. But the noise, the joy, the song made my mind up for me, and I got out of the car and stood there, swept up in the moment.

The organiser was good at her job. At each picket line, once she had set the *toyi-toying* going, she would *toyi-toyi* for a while herself. Then she would seek out the lead shop steward, go into a huddle with her, and, once she was sure that all was well, we would move on to the next factory.

At one factory, a large five-storey brick building with those typical factory windows made up of square panes of glass in metal frames, there were very few people near the building's doors, and the organiser looked worried. But after a quick word with a woman standing nearby, she indicated the factory doors to me and we went inside. As we climbed the wide concrete stairs, we could hear singing. And as we reached the factory canteen on the third floor and pushed open a pair of massive swinging doors, we were hit by the sound. The canteen was filled with hundreds of people *toyi-toying* and singing.

The lead shop steward was a woman of huge energy. She had a portable set of steps, from which she was encouraging the *toyi-toying* by singing and shouting through a megaphone. At the sight of the organiser, she came down the steps and they talked briefly together. I could see the shop steward glance two or three times at me and, after a minute or two, the two of them approached me. Using the organiser as interpreter, the shop steward asked me to address the crowd. Here I made a mistake that I have regretted ever since. I refused. Why? Because I was Australian? White?... I do not know, but I stood there saying that I was an outsider, not part of this, I supported it of course, but it was not my place… The shop steward lost interest in my babbling, dragged me to the foot of the steps, made me stand there, climbed the steps, shouted through her loudspeaker for quiet, and then spoke volubly in Zulu. The crowd looked at me and there was a deafening roar of applause. The shop steward spoke again, and there was an even more deafening roar of laughter.

The crowd took up their *toyi-toying* again, and I moved back to the organiser, who was still laughing. I asked her what had happened, and she explained that the shop steward had said, 'We have a comrade who has come all the way from Australia to support our strike.' That was when there was the roar of applause. And the shop steward had gone on, 'But he is too frightened to speak to you!' That, of course, was when there was the laughter.

Sight, sound, a welter of thoughts and emotions, joy, hope, inspiration. Other things happened on that day. A factory manager, male and white, appeared before hundreds of *toyi-toying* women, all of whom were black. He asked for a moment's silence, and told them that the pay office was open for another half hour for those who had not yet collected their pay for the week before the strike. The encounter was conducted with civility, respect and goodwill on both sides, and he was encouraged to stay for a moment while the picketers serenaded him. I watched a white woman, one of the administrative staff, cross a picket line of about forty *toyi-toying* workers. On their invitation, she paused for a minute or two and *toyi-toyied* with them. The women at another factory *toyi-toyied* towards us, singing a song composed for the occasion. It was in Zulu but each verse ended with the very recognisable words in English: 'Ten per cent'.

Alone in a Sharpeville shebeen

Halfway through my stay in Jo'burg, I was taken to Sharpeville, a black township about ninety kilometres south of Johannesburg. Thirty-six years earlier, on 21 March 1960, there was a demonstration in Sharpeville, and as the demonstrators approached the police station, the police opened fire, killing sixty-eight women, children and men, and injuring another hundred and eighty. The massacre is fixed in South African history. The date is now a public holiday for human rights. Nelson Mandela, the prisoner turned president, chose the township as the site where he signed the country's post-apartheid constitution on 11 December 1996.

There were five of us in the car for the day in Sharpeville: Bandile, two women organisers from the teachers' union, another COSATU official, and me. We visited the site of the Sharpeville shootings. The police station seemed unchanged from the photos I remembered seeing in Sydney newspapers at the time. We visited different parts of the township, cruising the unsurfaced streets lined with typical 'matchbox' houses. We stopped at a house where we drank soft drink, listened to local music on a state-of-the-art sound system, and talked. Late in the afternoon, we drove to a shebeen.

A shebeen is an unofficial and/or illegal drinking house. The one we entered had no signage outside, so you had to know it was there. We entered through a door in a wall, and went down two steps into a covered courtyard. There was a bar to one side, and a scatter of tables and chairs. There were fifteen or so people there and they fell silent when we entered. I was, after all, the only white person there and, for all I knew, in all of Sharpeville. But I was with Bandile, who was known both locally and nationally, and, after a pause, the other patrons of the shebeen lost interest in me and went back to their drinking and talking. The other man in our group went to the bar and returned with beers for all five of us, and we, too, got on with our drinking and talking.

Throughout the day, my comrades had spoken in English. Now they conferred in Zulu, but the moment was brief. Shortly after that, Bandile said he had seen a friend he needed to talk to and he left the table. Shortly after that. the other COSATU official said much the same, and he left the table. And shortly after that. our two women comrades said they were going to the toilets, and they left the table. Suddenly I was alone.

I began to feel uncomfortable. I assume that I presented no problem to anyone who had seen our group arrive. But new people were arriving as the shebeen filled, and I could see them pause as they came through the door in the wall, surprised at the sight of a lone white man occupying one of the diminishing number of available tables. One or two looked astonished, one or two looked angry, and one or two looked positively hostile.

Had I been abandoned? What would I do if I had been abandoned? How would I get back to Johannesburg? Would I get back to Johannesburg? It was unlikely that there were taxis cruising the streets outside looking for white people to take back to Johannesburg. Was there a bus service? Would whoever was running the shebeen help?

Bandile returned to the table, quickly followed by the other three. And I calmed down. Now that I could think rationally again, I realised that I had been alone at the table for not much more than five minutes. And when I looked keenly at my comrades, were all four of them smiling?

Spending social capital in Jo'burg

Some social theorists talk about a 'civil society' based on trust. They argue that we can accumulate trust, and they call this accumulation 'social capital'. So a neighbour and I might agree to take turns checking on an elderly woman in our street. If my neighbour and I keep to our agreement, we become ready to trust each other in other matters as well. Eva Cox, a social theorist who wrote a small and profound book entitled *A truly civil society*, argues that, unlike other forms of capital, the more social capital we spend, the more we amass.

Near the end of my time in Jo'burg, Bandile took me to a jazz club, where I witnessed people of all hues going about constructing a civil society out of what for forty years had been a truly uncivil society. I had a cold and made noises about getting a reasonably early night. As it was, we stayed the full evening (although I am told I fell asleep on at least one occasion) and my companions delivered me back to my hotel in the early hours of the morning.

When we arrived at the club, there were only a few people there. Bandile and I joined four others who were already sitting at a table. We talked and drank beer. Gradually, people arrived, mostly in couples or small groups. There seemed, apart from my table, to be very few racially mixed groups. By the time the band assembled, a reasonable crowd, made up of marginally more black people than white, had gathered.

The South African Jazz Pioneers were a band of six pieces – guitar, piano, saxophone, trumpet, trombone and drums – and a singer. The influences were eclectic – swing, traditional jazz, pop, modern chamber jazz, and black South African. The lead singer was a rake-like man, dressed in a dark, conventional suit. He looked so fragile that I wondered whether he would last the first song, let alone the whole evening, but he sang, switching from Zulu to English and back, with a subdued but unflagging energy.

The first bracket was long, musically complex, and very good. People drank quietly and listened. One person, a black woman, danced. She got up from a table after a couple of songs and moved close to the band, and then danced by herself, unselfconsciously, smiling from time to time at members of the band or at her friends. During a fast final number, some of the crowd cheered her on, and she got a round of applause as she went back to her table and sat down.

The beer and the quality of the music made me forget my cold, and we stayed on. The room became noisier, and considerably more people had arrived by the time the band took up their positions for the second and final bracket of the evening. This time, the music was tougher, the phrasing more marked, and more of the numbers carried the rhythms and harmonies of music from the townships. The sole dancer from the first bracket was on her feet again, but this time there were others as well, in particular a white woman. She danced alongside the black woman for a while, and then began inviting others to get up and dance. The black woman joined her and together they moved from table to table, pulling people to their feet. The women at our table were moving to the music and suddenly they jumped up and dragged a white woman at the next table, shy and demure-looking, to her feet. Bandile followed them. Others jumped up, blacks dragging whites to their feet, whites dragging blacks. For a while, it seemed that women invited women to dance and men simply followed the women from their table, but after a while this slight reserve broke down and men invited women and women men until everyone in the club was dancing.

As an outsider, I cannot be sure how spontaneous the actions of those two women were, but the evening now had an exhilaration about it that was more than one gets when simply drinking and dancing to excellent music. Only a few years ago, such an interracial event would have been illegal. Now, as far as I could see, everyone had become involved in a celebration of the new normality, and was engaged in a profligate expenditure of trust.

Farewelling my father-in-law

I came across an elegantly written article by a philosopher called Steven Segal in which, after Bauman and Heidegger, he drew a distinction between enemies and strangers. Enemies may oppose us, but they accept the same terms of reference as we do. They are from the same world as us. Strangers, on the other hand, are far more threatening. They are from another world altogether, and we cannot anticipate how they will think or how they will behave.

I do not want to apply his ideas too strictly, but in Segal's terms, Mathilde was my enemy. She intervened between my children and me, sometimes literally standing in my way. She contradicted what I said. She criticised me to Marianne. When we were in France, she would make decisions about the children that she should not have made – about what they should wear, about what they should do for the day, about when to call a doctor… But I knew what she was doing. And I could do it because Mathilde and I knew each other. We skirmished across a terrain that was familiar to both of us.

Achille, however, was a stranger to me. He and I existed in different political and philosophical realms, and I never really knew him. On the rare occasions that he and I were alone together, we were profoundly ill at ease.

Achille was a man of strong moral conviction. Show the slightest sign of weakness and he was quick to judge. Some people of his generation would have seen this moral rigidity as evidence that he was 'an honourable man'. I could not understand it. And if I didn't understand Achille, he didn't understand me. When I was working as a community education worker in London (*animateur de quartier* would be the closest French equivalent), he explained me away to his friends as a teacher of

English literature. And our conversations were always strained. Achille could not let a grammatical error pass by without correcting me, which meant he was not listening to what I was saying, but only to whether I was saying it correctly.

I was in New York when Achille died. It was 1994. I had been to a conference in Washington and had gone on to New York to see Alicia. Marianne phoned Alicia's tiny apartment and left a message on her answerphone. Achille's condition had suddenly worsened… Marianne had flown directly from Sydney to Paris and had got there just in time to say goodbye.

Alicia and I decided to fly to Paris as soon as possible. Alicia had no trouble booking a ticket because she is half-French and had a French as well as an Australian passport. I, on the other hand, needed a visa. I rang the French consulate in New York, and was told to go to their offices on Manhattan's upper east side. I did and, although there was no one else in the waiting room, I was made to wait.

Relationships between France and Australia were not good at the time. France had conducted a series of nuclear tests in the Pacific ending in 1991, and they were gearing up for yet another set of tests beginning in 1995. There had been demonstrations outside the embassy in Canberra and the consulates in the major Australian cities. Things had gone too far. The tyres of French-made cars had been slashed. French restaurants had been boycotted. Ridiculous…

I sat there in the consulate and my paranoia gradually increased. As closing time approached, I was told to come back the next morning. Would they 'lose' my passport overnight? Alicia flew out for Paris. I stayed on in New York, *sans* passport. I reported back to the consulate early the next day. Again, they made me wait. Finally, reunited with my passport, I headed for the airport.

My plane flew overnight and touched down at Charles de Gaulle airport shortly after six a.m. I walked through passport control and am pretty sure the laid-back officer did not look beyond the first page to see whether I had a visa or not. I collected my bag from the carousel, and headed for the exit. I had intended to take the RER into Paris, but Michel was standing there. Michel is married to Marianne's oldest friend. The two women have known each other since they were infants. I have known Michel since 1967.

Michel drove me into Paris, to the sixteenth arrondissement, but instead of turning into the street where the apartment of my parents-in-law was, he drove on and parked outside a busy brasserie.

'You don't want to go to the apartment yet,' he told me.

The French do things differently. In Australia, the funeral people take the body of the deceased away pretty quickly. In Franc, they tidy the body up and leave it neatly arranged in the house or apartment so that friends and family can visit it. Michel was right. I did not want to go to the apartment just yet.

We went into the brasserie and ate a breakfast of rich, beautiful coffee served in large bowls, and crisp, perfectly textured croissants. We talked, and sometime later Michel suggested a port or cognac. The French do not obsess about the sun having to be over the yardarm. Other patrons do not purse their lips.

By about eleven a.m., I was ready to face the family and make my farewells to Achille. Michel dropped me off. I took the lift, pushed on the apartment buzzer, and Marianne opened the door.

The day of the funeral was a full one. There was a church service mid-morning. The French navy does not forget its own. Two officers arrived with flags, and stood motionless throughout the service, holding the flags so that they hung directly above the coffin.

Alicia had asked to speak, and she began her short funeral oration with these words: *'Mon grand-père etait un homme dur*. My grandfather was a hard man.'

'Dear god,' I thought. 'She's doing a warts and all.' But I was misjudging our daughter. Alicia and Achille had developed a deep and loving relationship, which she now described. They had gone for long walks together in the streets of Paris, and in the hills surrounding the village in the south. They had read poetry together, and Achille had written poetry addressed to her. Alicia's love for her grandfather was evident, and people were moved.

After the service, the family, several close family friends and the priest drove in a convoy out of Paris. We lunched in a village restaurant, and then went on to a cemetery, bordered by a forest on one side and farmland on the other three. Achille was buried in a short ceremony conducted by the priest. From there, we went to a hunting chateau in the forest. The chateau belonged to friends of the family. The front section was pure eighteenth century. To the rear were the outbuildings and an untidy yard typical of any working farm. I remember members of our party, all dressed in black, in the last light of the day, walking in quiet contemplation in the garden in front of the chateau. We ate a simple meal, prepared by the couple who managed the farm, and then drove back into Paris.

I want to go back to the church service. When Marianne and I entered the church, our eldest nephew placed me next to my mother-in-law in the front pew, and took Marianne with him into the pew directly behind. When the service was over, Mathilde stood, unsteadily, and held on to me for support. She and I then walked down the central aisle to the door, where she asked me to stand beside her, and readied herself to acknowledge people as they left the church. Were we, I wondered, engaged in an unspoken reconciliation?

I found myself shaking hands with friends of the family (most of whom I knew from dinners and parties over the years at the house in the south), former naval officers including an admiral, and people I had never laid eyes on before. The friends talked to me for a moment before moving on to talk at more length to Mathilde. The people who did not know the family well addressed me, saying well-meant but platitudinous things such as 'my condolences to you and your family, monsieur'.

For a moment, I wondered why I was performing this role of greeting the mourners, then understood. Jean-Claude, my brother-in-law, had died four years earlier. Now Achille was gone. That left me as the oldest male in the family and, in accordance with some ancient patriarchal custom, sentiments directed to the whole family were now more properly addressed to me.

Having written the above, I am no longer so sure that Segal's distinction works. I miss Achille, and you can't miss a stranger, can you?

I have a strong memory of driving Achille and Mathilde from the family house in the village of Rocbaron to a dinner party in Toulon. I dropped them off and watched them walk across the street to the front gate of their friends' house. Both Achille's parents had been Corsican, and Achille had that long, strong, handsome face you see in Corsica. In old age, he held himself erect, unbowed. And Mathilde? She looked with undimmed pride at her man.

Circus in Laurieton

Alicia came home from New York and proceeded to work as a circus performer for the next twelve years. She stayed with the one circus – Circus Monoxide – for all of that time.

Circus Monoxide's first manifestation was at the Bathurst car races, hence the name, which stuck. It was 'new circus'. It did not have animals, or a traditional ringmaster, or clowns with floppy shoes and red-noses. Alicia was the circus clown, but her clowns were a collection of characters. Over the years, some died off, others were born, but they included Rodney, an embittered entertainer who had been thrown off the cruise liners for some unspecified but no doubt dreadful act. He would rail at the audience about being reduced to master of ceremonies of this hick outfit, and he tended to drift into blue material by mistake... I realise this sounds inappropriate for a circus, but the small kids loved Rodney, and would shout out his name whenever he appeared.

Another of Alicia's clowns was Maria, an irrepressibly cheerful latin-American. She, too, was greeted by shouts of joy from tiny voices. And another was a bathing belle. She was delivered into the ring in a suitcase. She got out, turned on a tap on the inside of the suitcase lid, filled the suitcase with water (which, of course was impossible), and then bathed in it. This act ended with the bathing belle diving deep into the suitcase and emerging with a string of pearls. She then packed herself back into the suitcase (which, of course, was impossible) and was wheeled away.

Alicia was not an aerialist but she did occasionally end up in the air. Rodney, for example, would look for a seat, sit down on what turned out to be the trapeze bar, and be hauled up to the top of the tent, where he would hang upside down by his ankles and do a lot of angry shouting.

It was Christmas time in 1995 and our family was dispersed. Marianne was spending a month in Paris. Our son Frank was off with two mates, surfing the southern side of Java. Alicia was on tour. And I was doing nothing much in Sydney.

Alicia rang me, and I was saying all the above when she said, 'Stop whingeing and come and spend a few days with the circus. We're in Laurieton. It's beautiful. There's a campsite close by and you can get a cabin there.'

I drove out of Sydney a couple of hours later, and into Laurieton mid-morning the next day. Alicia was right. The place was beautiful. The town was backed up against an odd, abrupt mountain with an impressive rock face, and a cluster of small trees on the top. The town centre was a small grid of streets near a lagoon and a beach. To get to the lagoon, you walked down a slope to a well-kept sports ground, then across an unsurfaced road to a patch of lawn next to the water. The circus was pitched there, some fifty metres from a boatshed.

Over its fourteen years on the road, the circus went through a number of changes, from a small affair with no wall or tent, to a mid-sized affair with a canvas wall but still open to the stars, to the full deal with a big top, made by specialist tent makers just outside Venice.

The circus I walked towards in Laurieton was in that first phase, and from a distance it looked like a camp of travellers. There was an old double-decker bus, a van and a car parked in an apparently haphazard way, objects were scattered across the lawn, and scruffily dressed people were wandering around. As you got closer, however, you could see the bus was acting as a backdrop to a canvas ring laid out on the grass, and that the grass had white markings on it. There were steel poles and supporting cables to hold the lights and the trapeze for the aerialists. The objects lying about were a collection of hoops, a large ring, a small platform for a tap dance act, and a collection of juggling clubs. The people were not aimlessly wandering about. They were in the middle of their morning rehearsals. Alicia waved.

I rented a cabin for three nights in the campsite close by, and offered my services to the circus. To my delight, they said I could help by videoing the next three performances so that they could review and make changes to their program. And so, for the three days, I became a member (even if a very ancillary one) of the troupe.

People began wandering down from the town and across the playing field while it was still light. The performers would be in the ring dressed any-old-how, standing about chatting, rehearsing tricks, stretching their bodies, and gradually warming up. Since there was no tent or wall, people arriving early sat on the grass and watched.

As the light in the sky was going, going, something would happen behind the audience, and in the instant that people looked round, the performers were gone. In the moment of surprise that followed, one the performers would stand up from amongst the people sitting on the grass, walk into the ring and begin warming the audience up. While he was pointing to where someone might sit, a red handkerchief would appear in his hand. He would push it back into his sleeve and it would appear in his other hand. He got the kids to practise cheering, and the adults clapping, by joining his hands, holding them low, and trying to jump over them. He kept falling over and bouncing upright. Finally he succeeded, and in the cheering that followed, something – a shout, or a single clash of cymbals somewhere in the surrounding dark – would happen and when people looked back, the ring was bathed in light, the three musicians were in place and playing, the performers were in full costume, and a wild tumbling act by the whole company was under way.

The final act was a hat act. All the performers came into the ring wearing different-shaped hats, which they would swap, steal, and throw into the air and catch on their heads, with ever increasing speed. The act ended with them standing in a line, holding the hats upside down.

One of them would say over the sound system, 'We do this for a living. If you had taken the kids for a pizza, you would have spent about twenty dollars. That's the kind of contribution we're looking for. So come into the ring, pop the money into a hat, and talk to us.'

And another voice would say, 'And if you don't have the money, come in and talk to us anyway.'

Circus Monoxide established an intimacy with their audiences. The audience was close in to the ring, and the performers spoke directly to them, sometimes addressing an individual, sometimes picking out a family group, or a couple. For some of the acts, the performers called for volunteers, and for others, they invited the audience to shout out warnings, or cheers of encouragement. All of which meant that, when they invited the audience to come into the ring at the end of the show, people did.

This was a magical moment. One of the performers would give out posters with plenty of white space on them, and textas, and the kids would run around collecting autographs. The jugglers would give the kids impromptu lessons. The musos would let the kids play with an old ukelele they kept for that purpose. And with the permission of the parents, the taller of the two aerialists might hold some of the smaller kids up and let them hang from the trapeze bar.

Little by little, the audience would drift away and when, finally, they had all gone, someone would reduce the lighting to a single light above the ring, and a ritual would follow. The musos would open a bottle of wine, each take a glass and wander off in different directions into the darkness. The performers would wander away as well until each felt comfortably distanced from the ring, and there they would do cooling down exercises, stretching gently, sitting and checking their muscles, turning their heads.

On my last evening with the circus, I asked if I could accompany one of the two aerialists, and I sat on the grass a little distance from her, and felt the warmth and the darkness envelop me. I could hear the lapping of water in the lagoon a few metres from us, and had a sense, but please do not ask me to articulate it, of what kept these circus people going.

The eight performers and the three musos all took turns cooking for a day. The upper level of the double-decker bus was sleeping quarters, and the lower level had seating for when it rained, and a kitchen. The cook for the day called everyone back into the light, put the small tap dancing platform in the middle of the ring and brought the meal from the bus. People came in from the surrounding darkness, bringing with them their calm and their silence, and sat round the platform, and ate.

I was invited to eat with them and, on each of the three evenings I was there, the meal continued for some time in silence.

Finally, someone would speak. 'I thought the timing wasn't good in the Top of the Town.' (That was the opening tumbling act.)

'Yeah, it could have been tighter.'

'And I don't think we got the transition from Wimbledon to the Bathing Belle right.' (Wimbledon was a juggling act.)

Now people were talking, and planning what they would concentrate on when they assembled for their regular rehearsal at nine the next morning. Be they glassblowers, concert pianists, firefighters, bricklayers, or circus people, there is something special about seeing professionals at work.

PS: The Circus Monoxide troupe might have looked scruffy on first encounter but, when the lights came on and the performance was under way, the quality of their work was unmistakable. The aerialist who let me sit nearby as she did her cooling down exercises is Chelsea McGuffin. She was not much more than twenty at the time and already very skilled. Twenty-odd years on and she has a reputation as the compleat circus performer, and is in high demand nationally and internationally. She can work on a high wire, come dropping and spinning (almost) to earth on a tissue, tumble and, in an acrobatics act called 'toss the girl', she can fly!

Wild weather over Dorrigo

Over the years, we put a number of circus performers up at our house in Sydney. Alicia would phone ahead, saying that Gareth would be in Sydney and could we help? Gareth built a tower of chairs and then climbed to the top of the tower, made red handkerchiefs appear and disappear, juggled and played a mean banjo. He would install himself in our back garden and play quietly to himself for hours. On one occasion, he came with Paddy, who did trapeze.

Marianne took Paddy to her room and left her, saying we would be having something to eat in the garden in twenty minutes or so. Marianne joined Gareth and me and we waited. And waited. Marianne went back into the house and emerged a few minutes later saying that there was no sign of Paddy.

I said, 'Did anyone hear the front door being opened and closed?'
No one had.

I went and looked up and down the street. Paddy was nowhere to be seen. I went back through the house to the garden. The four of us began eating.

A few minutes later, Paddy emerged from the house. She sat down. Marianne handed her a plate and she began eating.

Up to that moment, I had not heard Paddy utter a single word. I let her get on with her meal, and when she was finished I leant forward and said, 'Where were you?'

Paddy explained. 'I went up into your attic bedroom and out through the dormer window,' she said. 'I climbed up to the peak of the roof. I was sitting there and lost track of time.'

Alicia told us that Paddy was like that. The circus had been pitched in the showground at Dorrigo and the steel frames for the trapeze and the lights had been set up. Circus Monoxide was in its second phase and had a canvas wall, but was still open to the sky and dependent on the weather. Alicia said that Paddy spent a lot of her time sitting on the highest point of the steel frame and that, when a thunderstorm passed over them, with sudden gusts of wind, heavy rain and flashes of lightning, she had to plead with Paddy to come down and take shelter in the bus. When Paddy joined them, her clothes were soaked, her hair was hanging down in strands and her eyes were shining.

Boff!

I want to say a little more about Andrew Fisher (and others).

Andrew could offer excellent advice. He had a law degree from the University of Sydney and a masters degree in international law from the University of London, a vast store of general knowledge and a canny way of reading people. A number of Australians rose to prominence in London in the 1960s. I've already mentioned Richard Neville, Jim Anderson and Martin Sharp. Marsha Rowe was a leading force in founding the feminist magazine *Spare Rib*, Alex Mitchell was making his mark as an investigative journalist with the *Sunday Times*, Bruce Beresford was making his first feature movie, and Germaine Greer was writing *The Female Eunuch*.

A number of these people owed their success in some part to Andrew's advice and encouragement. Andrew, however, was unable to heed his own advice, and both his professional life and his love life were chaotic.

Back in Sydney in the 1980s and 1990s, Marianne and I grew accustomed to Andrew's leaden tread on our front steps heralding his arrival and his announcement that his most recent adventure of the heart had come to an end. There would follow a long and dispirited monologue full of damning self-assessment. Marianne would listen hard, and as Andrew neared the end of his monologue, she would shrug, and say that wonderful French word *Boff*. Andrew would pull himself together and say, 'At least I learnt a lot,' which patently he had not.

Boff is a kind of dismissal. It contains a touch of 'Who cares anyway' and 'It's not important'. It is an affectionate version of the English language phrase 'Get a life', but with any hint of condemnation removed. The speaker accompanies the word with a tilt of the head, rounds her or his lips, and pushes out a small bubble of air so as to make a light popping sound! So totally benign is the word *Boff* that the person being addressed will often respond in kind, and the newcomer to French is then treated to the spectacle of two adults blowing the smallest of raspberries at each other. Andrew found it difficult to respond to Marianne's *Boff* other than by laughing.

Accosted in Kingston, Jamaica

I was in Jamaica in the mid-1990s, and the people hosting my visit told me that I was not to take a bus from the airport, and that I must use one particular taxi company and no other. I was to make sure the taxi doors were locked. I was to take the taxi directly to the visitors' residence on the Mona Campus of the University of the West Indies, on the edge of Kingston. And I was to stay on the campus. I was tired and went straight to bed, so it was only the next morning that I realised that I was both a guest of the university and its prisoner.

At first, I complied with my hosts' instructions, but my frustration grew, and I began playing hooky. I went for a short walk off campus and returned alive. I took a longer walk with the same result. On a free evening, instead of eating in the visitors' residence bar, I ordered a taxi (from the approved company) and asked the driver to take me to a restaurant. He took me to a large building, a former colonial home whose ground floor and gardens had been converted into a covered pedestrian precinct with restaurants and shops – the sort of place you find all over the world.

My visit was more than half over and, apart from two taxi rides and that precinct, I had not seen anything of the town. On the tourist map there was a section of Kingston called 'Downtown', a collection of narrow streets and what looked like a town square. From the map and the name, I assumed it would be the most interesting part of the city, but I had received very strict instructions: 'Do not go to Downtown.' All right, but north of Downtown was an area of hotels with internationally familiar names, and I thought that if I took a taxi to one of them, then I could walk towards Downtown, monitoring my surroundings carefully, and turn back if it did look like I was approaching a no-go area.

I paid the taxi, and instead of entering the hotel, turned and started in the direction of Downtown. I had walked a very short distance and was still in sight of the hotel when I found myself accosted by three men. One, wearing the most amiable of smiles, was standing directly in front of me, the other two were positioned on either side and a little to the rear of me. I glanced at my new sidekicks and they were not smiling. The leader told me that he had some excellent dope that he was sure I would want to buy.

I understood that refusing to hand over whatever money I had on my person would be foolhardy. But I also understood that accepting the dope would put me beyond the law. I hesitated, and the dealer on my left began speaking vehemently in a patois I could not understand. I remembered seeing a Jamaican film in London years before that was entirely in patois, and being thankful that it had subtitles. The other two dealers replied in patois and a discussion, no doubt about what to do with me, followed.

The leader turned his attention back to me and made it clear that I had to pay up. To do so, he shifted back from patois into a standard form of English that I had no trouble understanding, so I said, 'Do you know the score?'

'What are you talking about, man?'

'The cricket. West Indies is playing Pakistan, in Kingston, at Sabina Park.'

'You're not American?'

'I'm Australian.'

At that time, the Australian cricket team was acknowledged as the best in the world, so I hastened on, 'Our team is good at the moment but it's nothing compared to the brilliant team you blokes had back in the 1970s and 1980s.' I searched for names, and motivated by fear, found some. 'We don't have batsmen like Gordon Greenidge and Desmond Haynes or Richards and Richardson, or Clive Lloyd. And what about your bowlers? Do you remember Malcolm Marshall. You're old enough,' I said to the dealer on my right. 'Marshall was magnificent.

When he got a wicket, he would run down the pitch, waving his finger like this.' And I demonstrated, waving my index finger in small circles.

The mood changed. All three joined in the conversation, each one using standard English. No subtitles needed.

A moment came when one of the sidekicks, who may not have been as big a cricket tragic as the other two, said something like, 'Oh, fook it, mun' and turned away from me.

I took this to mean that our encounter was over, and I walked as steadily as I could back to the hotel and this time I went in. I found a swimming pool to the rear of the lobby with a poolside bar. It was still quite early in the day but an agreeable barman served me a Scotch and I sat there on a stool, watching wealthy people, some of them tall and beautiful, at play.

When a colleague heard I was going to the West Indies, he had said, 'When all else fails, talk about the cricket.' But I think he was talking about awkward social silences rather than criminal transactions and muggings.

PS: Some years later, I heard a linguist give a paper in which she argued that there was no single English language but rather a vast number of versions of English, each one a legitimate language in itself. What is more, she argued, none of these myriad versions could claim to be better than any other, or have any authority over any other. There was no such thing as an official or standard English.

I collared her after her paper. 'Are you sure?' I asked her.

'Of what?' she said.

'Of your major thesis, that there is no standard English.'

'Quite sure,' she said,

And so I told her how my drug dealer associates in Jamaica had discussed what to do with me in a patois I had no hope of understanding, and yet employed a standard English, which all four of us understood and could use, when it came to celebrating the genius of the West Indies cricket teams of the 1970s and 1980s.

'You haven't understood my paper,' she said.

'Hang on,' I said. 'What if your paper's at fault, and not me? Aren't you blaming the victim?'

She stared at me for a moment, looking as if she wanted to poke me in the eye, but there were others waiting to speak to her and she turned towards them.

Seeing the sights in Jamaica

My stay in Jamaica was coming to an end and I still had not seen much of Kingston, or any of the countryside outside the city. I hired a taxi for the one full day I had left and told the driver, whose name was Danny, that I wanted to see different parts of Kingston and, if possible, the part on the map called Downtown. When we had done that, I wanted him to take me into the mountains behind Kingston, maybe finding somewhere up there for lunch, and then let me see a bit more of the mountains before heading back into Kingston. I told him I had had a few busy days and I wanted to sit back in the car and relax. He was happy with the plan, and the US fifty-dollar fee he was charging me. We set off.

Danny took me to various parts of Kingston and explained who controlled them. It seemed that it was sometimes a member of parliament, or a tycoon of sorts, or a gang, or an individual gangster. It sounded complicated. He took me to Downtown but it was disappointing. I had been hoping for houses centuries old. Perhaps they were there but I saw none. There was a large and colourful market but Danny would not let me out of the car.

Around midday, Danny said he would take me into the mountains to a resort where I could eat. The drive would take about forty-five minutes to an hour. We were driving along a short street at the time, and having got my OK, he took the next turn to the left. The road we entered was some three hundred metres long, with low housing and a number of vacant allotments. As we entered the street, he slowed the car, reached under the driver's seat and took out a circular shield. He held the shield up between his head and the driver's window, and then drove like a bat out of hell. The street ended in a T-intersection, and he turned right and slowed down. He put the shield back under the seat, and we drove through the outer suburbs of Kingston and into the mountains.

Danny said nothing and I said nothing. It was all over so quickly that it might not have happened. I sat there, aghast. 'What about me?' I thought. 'Where was my shield?' Then I began thinking more clearly. The shield Danny held up would have been useless against a bullet. It must, therefore, have been to hide his identity. Had we been in a part of Kingston controlled by a gangster, or a gang, or a tycoon, or a member of parliament he had affronted in some way?

By the time I had settled down, we were on the mountain road, which was steep and narrow, and I was fearful of distracting him with any questions. And by the time we reached the mountain resort, I was eager to eat – comfort eat, you could say, and you would be right – and we had both lapsed into a state of denial.

After lunch, Danny drove me down the mountainside and back to the university campus where I was staying. We talked of inconsequential things on the way, and when we pulled up in front of the university's visitors' residence, we shook hands, smiled at each other and said goodbye. I had a drink that evening in the residence bar, but did not feel inclined to talk about my experience.

I had spent more than a week in Jamaica but had learnt very little. I had let myself be governed by others' fear, and my own, and it was too late to remedy it.

A multicultural send-off

Mathilde hated Germans with a passion. She had lived through the German occupation of France during the Second World War. She saw Occupation authorities ejecting a pregnant Jewish patient from the hospital where she (Mathilde) gave birth to Marianne. This explains the first part of her response when Marianne announced that she was going to marry an Australian.

'At least, her mother said, 'he is not a German…' But it does not explain the other part, '…or a Jew.' Mathilde was appalled that the Jewish woman was being thrown out of the hospital, but still harboured a prejudice against Jewish people in general.

There were others who were swept up into my mother-in-law's ample net of disapproval. Mathilde ruled over the family house in the south of France, and on the few occasions when she left the house for any time at all, she would issue detailed instructions. Normally, this stream of instructions was directed at Laetitia and Marianne, but on one occasion, when she was leaving for three days to visit friends on the coast, she turned to me and said, 'Now, Mi-kol, you can invite anyone you like – Jews, Arabs, blacks and any other peculiar people.' (In French, the phrase flows much more smoothly: *les juifs, les arabs, les negres et les gens bizarres*.) I suppose it was intended as a joke, but doesn't that just make it worse?

Stay with me. This highlight jumps about a bit. In 1976, both my parents-in-law came to London and spent a week with us. It was a tough old time. Marianne was beginning to carve out a career in the Inner London Education Authority as a trainer of language teachers. She was working close to full time, and we had to put up with Mathilde repeatedly saying that Marianne was a bad mother and that no woman could work and still manage to raise children properly. Achille did not intervene, and so I was glad to see the back of both of them when they got into a taxi and headed for Victoria station, and the train and ferry back to France. (The Eurostar was still some way off.)

They left about ten a.m. and three or so hours had passed when there was a knock on the door. I answered it and my father-in-law was standing there, without my mother-in-law. He came in and sat down and explained that in the crowds on the platform he and Mathilde had been separated. He looked for her but could not find her. He had both passports, both tickets and all their money, and so he was sure she would not get on the train without him. My mother-in-law, it transpired, assumed that her husband would have got on board. After all, he had the passports and the tickets and all the money and so would have had no reason to stay on the platform if she was on the train. Whatever the logic (or lack of it) in either's reasoning, the train drew out of Victoria station with Mathilde moving from carriage to carriage looking for her husband, and Achille standing on the platform, looking around him and expecting…what? His wife's lifeless body slumped sideways on one of the platform benches? His wife trussed up and with a gag in her mouth, being wheeled away on a porter's trolley by a couple of gangsters?

After walking the length of the train, Mathilde was forced to recognise that her husband was not on board. By that time, she was close to panic. She asked a British Rail guard for help, but he had no French and she had no English. Being a supplicant would not have sat easily with her and, despite her distress, she may have played *la grande dame*, asserting that she was the wife of a naval officer and that everybody around her should stop whatever they were doing and come to her aid. In any event, the guard turned his back and walked away, and she slumped into a vacant seat. I like to think that she had visions of sleeping on the Folkstone platform until kicked out of the station by transport police, of begging for money in the streets and being moved on, and of being arrested and put in a cell (oh yes) for trying to get on a train back to London without a ticket.

A man in his fifties had overheard my mother-in-law's appeal to the guard for help. Unlike the guard, he spoke French. He introduced himself and offered to help. 'When we get to Folkestone we will need to telephone your daughter,' he said, or words to that effect. 'Do you have her number? No? Do you know your daughter's address? *Gut.* Then we will get you on a return train to London. It will be my honour to buy you your ticket. I shall stay with you until your train leaves, and give you twenty-five British pounds for the taxi from Victoria Station to your daughter's house, in Shepherd's Bush, you say? *Gut.*'

Gut. Once Mathilde had calmed down and begun listening, she realised that her charming guardian angel spoke French with an accent she had heard in Paris during the Occupation, and that he was a German.

Back in London, we waited. As night closed in, we heard a taxi draw up outside, and my mother-in-law exploded into the house, half crying and ferociously angry with her husband.

We waved them off for a second time the next morning. Back in the house, I spent a moment looking at the phone. Would I lift the receiver off so that my parents-in-law would get an engaged signal if they got into further trouble and tried to ring us? But I didn't, and they didn't ring.

Stay with me again, this time as I jump forward some eighteen years. A year or so after the death of my father-in-law in 1994, Mathilde became bedridden. She did not want to move from her apartment to a home for the aged, and so the family arranged round-the-clock care. Laetitia and Marianne (on a trip by herself to Paris to do things just like this) turned the living room into a bedroom for their mother, and the bedroom and the study into two bedrooms equipped for students. They employed a woman from ten a.m. to six p.m. to do the shopping, clean the apartment, provide lunch and prepare an evening meal, and they offered free accommodation to two students in return for their caring for Mathilde overnight. The students could take turns to be on duty.

The woman who came during the day was Mauritian and was golden brown in colour. The two students, one doing a masters degree and the other a doctorate, were from west Africa, and were black and very black respectively. The three women developed an affection for my mother-in-law, to which she responded in kind, but it did not stop her saying to Marianne that fate had dealt her a terrible blow in forcing her to spend her last days in the company of three blacks.

What does one say to that? These women cater to your most intimate needs. You are comfortable with them. You smile and joke with them. They smile and joke with you. Why do you say such things?

Laetitia received a phone call very early in the morning from the doctoral student. Mathilde had died peacefully during the night. Laetitia dressed and went to her mother's apartment. She entered and heard some kind of singing. She went into her mother's room. The two students were kneeling on the floor, one chanting in her home language, the other wordlessly keening. Laetitia was moved and joined them in silent prayer.

Marianne climbed on a plane and headed for France for the funeral and, while Marianne was still somewhere in the air, Laetitia told me over the phone about the two women chanting and keening and her praying. It sounded like as nice a send-off as anyone, with the possible exception of my mother-in-law, could want.

PS: Where did Mathilde's knee-jerk racism come from? She was born in 1909 in Oran, the second city in Algeria. Her family were *pieds noirs*, that is, the white minority in control. They had Arab servants. Mathilde would have absorbed the racism of the gilded colonial society that surrounded her as easily, and unremarked, as drinking a glass of water.

Young women of good family in Oran played tennis with young officers from visiting French warships. It was a mating game. Achille and Mathilde met on a tennis court and some months later they married.

One would imagine that this would have taken Mathilde away from the enclosed community of her parents and their racism. Certainly it took her away from Algeria. As a naval officer's wife, she went first to the naval port of Brest in Brittany, and then to the naval port of Toulon on the Mediterranean. But that simply meant that she moved from one kind of racism to another.

It is now acknowledged that a number of the senior officers in the French navy in the 1930s were very right-wing. Mathilde would have heard strong expressions of anti-Semitism from some of Achille's fellow officers, and from some of their wives. Achille was young and wanted to please his superiors, and he did so by joining a right-wing organisation called Action française.

There is no point in sitting in judgement. Who knows what any of us would have done back there and then? Marianne tells me that Achille's membership of Action française was short lived.

And one last thing: Mathilde ignored the pressures from her social group and voted in the referendum of 1962 for the independence of Algeria. What's more, she said out loud that she had. Independent, brave…have I got Mathilde terribly wrong?

Meeting a good person in South Africa

During my 1996 visit to South Africa, I spent a fortnight attached to the Trade Union Research Centre (TERC) at the University of Kwazulu Natal, Durban. During my time there, I spent a morning in a squatters' camp on the edge of Durban. I gained entry through another visiting Australian. She had been at a bus stop in central Durban and had struck up a conversation with Sithando Ntshingila, a resident of Cato Crest squatters' camp. He had invited her to visit the camp, and she had invited me to accompany her.

The camp covered two sides of a small valley, a mass of dwellings inhabited by anything up to ten thousand people. Most of the dwellings were made from corrugated iron, mud and wood, and had floors of beaten earth.

Sithando met us at the edge of the camp and led us in along a winding path to his own dwelling, where we two visitors sat on a large comfortable sofa and Sithando sat in a large comfortable armchair opposite us. We talked.

Sithando was unemployed and told us he had no official position within the social structure of the camp. However, people had greeted him as we passed in a way that suggested he was much respected. He talked of life in the camp, of the struggle to get even the most basic facilities, and of the projects he had played a part in setting up. They included a car washing cooperative and a market gardens cooperative. He talked about a training program for unemployed people that had been established by the authorities with little or no community consultation.

And that led him to talk with a wry disillusion about the post-apartheid government bureaucrats from whom he tried to get funding. They were not markedly different from the old ones. 'They speak Zulu instead of English or Afrikaans now,' he said with a smile, 'but they still speak the same language.'

Sithando had limped as he led the two of us through the camp. And now that we sat facing each other and talking I could see that his right arm was all but useless and that he had to lift it with his left hand to place it across his lap or on the arm of the chair. He told us he had been active in the Young Christian Workers in the 1970s, and outspoken about workers' rights. He had been picked up by the police and warned to stop his activism. He had maintained his membership of the YCW and continued advocating its ideas. He had been picked up and warned again. Since nothing he was doing was unlawful, he had continued as before, and in 1984 he was picked up again. That time, he was beaten up. The beating was so brutal that he almost died, his right leg was permanently damaged, and his right arm paralysed.

Sitting opposite Sithando, listening to him, looking into his eyes, watching him smile, I knew I was in the presence of a good person. It is difficult to imagine the narrow-mindedness of those authorities who saw him as a threat to the state. And it is difficult to imagine the moral vacuum they must have lived in to beat him into permanent physical disability.

Sithando gave no details, but his beating was probably several beatings delivered by several people at a time. And there is a horrible – and admirable – irony about all this. The move from apartheid to post-apartheid government in South Africa happened by transition and not by revolution. There wasn't a period of summary justice and reprisals. Change was introduced slowly. When I met Sithando, it is just possible that some of the people who beat him might still have been in full-time employment in the South African police force.

No need for dismay in Khayelitsha

During my 2001 visit to South Africa, I was based for a fortnight in the Department of Adult Education at the University of Cape Town. I contributed to a course for community activists being run by Linda Cooper and Janice McMillan. A couple of days after my first meeting with the group, Linda told me she and Janice were going to visit three of the course participants who lived and worked in a township called Khayelitsha, some thirty kilometres from Cape Town. Would I like to come along?

I had visited Soweto and Sharpeville near Johannesburg, and Cato Crest Camp on the edge of Durban, but was still struck by the immensity of Khayelitsha, the lack of vegetation, the row upon row of matchbox houses, the dust from the unsurfaced roads – the unremitting harshness of it all. For the visitor from the comfortable places I inhabit, the crowded, cluttered, disordered landscape of low-lying constructions might well have come from a work of science fiction. (Since writing this, I have seen two science fiction films using South African townships as their locations.)

As if to reinforce this impression, there were anomalies. To get there, we had driven along a modern freeway. Once into the township, we got lost. We were looking for a petrol station at which we were to turn right, but found two in sight of each other, both with covered forecourts. The tilted covers, supported by thin metal stanchions, stood higher than the surrounding buildings so that the petrol stations, like two sentinels, dominated the landscape.

Once we had got our bearings, we drove to a building that housed the offices of a number of community agencies, where we found the three participants in Linda and Janice's course, and a community worker under whose guidance they were working. The six South Africans talked about unemployment, underemployment, the derisory wages that some of those in so-called employment actually received, petty crime, the cost of transport, and the perennial struggle for sufficient funding to do something about this array of problems.

I sat, silent, gradually overtaken by a sense of dismay. The sentiment grew. I had nothing to contribute. I could not imagine where anyone would start in order to repair the shocking inequities these people encountered every day.

I was still in Cape Town the following week, and Kholeka Ndamase, one of the course participants we had visited in Khayelitsha, said she wanted to talk with me after class. We took over Linda's office, and Kholeka asked me how she and her two colleagues might get started! My heart sank. Should I tell her that I did not know? Should I tell her about my dismay? Should I tell her that I was in the midst of an existential crisis?

I calmed down a little and thought. There is a form of social analysis in which we identify who are our friends and who are our enemies. Did Kholeka have friends and allies? I asked. Well, yes, her two colleague volunteers, the coordinator I had met, and some others. There was a whiteboard in Linda's office, and I suggested we indicate these people on the board and draw lines between them where the relationships were strong. What governed those relationships? Friendship? Family? Common experience? Beliefs? We wrote in one or two factors that mediated the relationships and drew some more lines. We went back to the first question. Did Kholeka have friends and allies? Yes, she did. And as a result of the exercise, she realised that she had a good number more.

So far, the individuals and organisations identified were allies. Were there any organisations or groups or individuals that Kholeka saw as likely to obstruct the programs she and her friends and allies might want to set up? That was a bit more difficult, but we put up one or two agencies that seemed indifferent to community initiatives, drew some lines to other agencies, and thought about what mediated those relationships. The whiteboard began looking untidy, but we could see some contacts that might be usefully reinforced, some new alliances to forge and several issues to explore.

It was late afternoon and Kholeka had to go. I sat for a while. We had not got very far. A few days later, I flew out of Cape Town and on to Europe and the next stage of my six months' study leave.

Some eighteen months later, it looked like I might get to South Africa again. In the end, I couldn't go and I wrote to Linda, telling her so. Linda added a postscript to her reply, saying that Kholeka would be disappointed. When Linda had told her that I might be visiting Cape Town again, Kholeka had said she would like me to visit the program for women she and her two colleagues were setting up.

PS: To the side of the community building in Khayelitsha was a cargo container donated by a shipping company and now housing a radio station. We were shown through a small door in the side of the container, and found ourselves in the antechamber to the broadcasting studio. On the other side of the glass panel in the studio itself, two announcers played township music, introduced with a patter in Xhosa replete with clicks. I did not understand a word, but the patter had the familiar swoops of intonation and extravagant emphases of the universal disc jockey.

A traveller's tale from Geneva

In 1996, I travelled by train from Paris to Geneva to interview two people at the International Labour Office, a UN agency with its headquarters there. I got into Geneva late in the afternoon and went to a tourist information desk at the station. They recommended a hotel within walking distance. The hotel was easy to find and I walked through the main entrance about ten minutes later.

The moment I was inside the hotel, I realised it was unnecessarily upmarket. All I needed was a bed and a shower. The hotel had a reception desk staffed by five or six people, porters waiting around, at least one posh-looking restaurant, and probably another one on another floor. There may have been a gym and a pool in the basement, for all I knew. I had come in from a busy street with shops bearing international fashion names, and I could see that the hotel stretched through to another street, and so I kept on walking. I emerged into the back street and turned right. Within the same block, I found a simple-looking hotel and I went in and booked a room.

The one person at the small reception desk asked me if I had company. He was reaching for a key on a panel of keys when he spoke, and his hand hesitated for a moment when I said, 'No.' He took a key down and handed it to me. I walked up two flights of stairs and found the room. It was not great, but it would do. I dropped my bag on the bed and made my way out of the hotel to have a first real look at Geneva. I wandered for a couple of hours and, when I began feeling hungry, found a restaurant and ate without hurry. It was dark when I turned back into the street where my hotel was located.

In the daylight, the street had looked nondescript, but with the night it had become the red-light district of Geneva. It was not a big red-light district, mind you, but for a stretch of about thirty metres the street was lined with sex workers. And my hotel was in the middle of it all. As I drew level with the first sex worker, she offered me a range of services on a climbing scale of prices. I replied that I was a resident at the hotel and not a potential client.

'He's a resident,' she shouted to the others. 'Don't waste your time on him. He's a resident.'

There was laughter.

I went into the hotel. There was no one at reception, so I suppose the workers paid the hotel in advance. I climbed the stairs. There was a couple climbing the stairs ahead me. I reached my room unaccosted and went in. I put the door on the chain and slept well.

The next day, I did my interviews at the ILO. I was introduced to others and treated to a lunch, and ended up spending a good part of the day there. When I got back into Geneva proper, it was late afternoon, and again I went wandering, found another restaurant and took my time over a light meal and a couple of glasses of wine. As I approached my hotel, I was greeted by the same sex worker, and again, for the benefit of anyone who had not been there the previous evening, she called out that I was a resident.

I do not want to leave you with the impression these were sex workers with hearts of gold, or that they were happy in their work. The evening before, I had put my head down and pushed ahead in order to get into the hotel. This time, I looked people in the eye and responded to the banter, and I could see that a number of the women had ravaged faces, and some were as thin as rakes. A couple of them were generous, in that they offered me services for free, although I am not such a fool as to think that they would not have then offered more services at the full price. I got to my room unscathed, slept well and took the train back to Paris the next morning.

Back at my university in Australia, I was required to write a report on the activities I had engaged in during my study leave. It went into the university's archives somewhere. And I was also required to present a paper to colleagues in my department. Making the presentation was compulsory, but attendance by my colleagues was not, and so it was necessary to find a title that caught people's attention. I submitted a small blurb to be circulated in the faculty under the title 'Mike Newman's nights in a Genevan brothel'.

I was in my office the next day when there was a light knock on the door and the head of school came in. He was holding the notice for my talk. 'Mike…' he said tentatively.

'Yes,' I said helpfully.

'Freda in administration does not think you are taking things seriously. In fact, she felt you were insulting her and her colleagues.'

'Oh dear, I didn't mean to do that,' I said, 'but you have to admit the title would get the punters in.'

The head of school was the gentlest of men and the most loyal of bosses, but he always got his way. He stood at the door, saying nothing. There was no point in resisting.

'All right, all right,' I said, 'I'll change it. What about "Workers' education: The International Labour Organisation's policies and practice"?'

'Perfect,' the head of school said.

I spoke to a throng of two colleagues, who seemed mainly interested in how to get cheap accommodation in Paris, and the head of school. You had to admire the doggedness of the man.

A small matter in Bangkok

I do not wear ties. For my wedding, yes, and my father-in-law's funeral, and one or two other occasions when not wearing a tie would have caused very real hurt, but other than that, I don't wear ties.

In 1998, I spent a week at Chulalongkorn University in Bangkok, as the guest of the Department of Informal Learning there. My Thai colleagues did not work me hard. In fact, they treated me like a privileged tourist. I was taken to visit a number of Buddhist temples in the city, and we went out of Bangkok for a day to visit a royal palace.

The only work I did for my hosts was to give a presentation to postgraduate students on different traditions of learning. I spoke in English. There was no interpreter, and I wondered whether anyone was following what I was saying. My unease was increased by a member of staff who moved around me as I spoke, taking photographs, like a member of the paparazzi pursuing someone mildly famous. I began to suspect that, in keeping with postmodern ideas of disconnectedness, the image of me standing in front of the group and talking was more real in the local scheme of things than anything I might be saying. I invited questions when I finished but no one responded. However. a couple of people whom I had talked to previously about their research did tell me that they had found my presentation useful, and I am ready to grab at any straw going.

My second last day in Thailand came, and my only duty was to report to the head of department's office at ten a.m., and then be taken to meet the dean of the faculty at ten fifteen. I saw this as no big deal. The dean of faculty in my university back in Sydney was a mate. We, and everyone else in the faculty, were on first name terms. The title 'dean' had some prestige, but not too much.

I knocked on the head's office door and went in. He had asked me to call him Jim when I first met him while he was visiting Sydney, which I had done. He was a man of considerable erudition, and well respected by his colleagues. He had studied for twelve years in the USA, returning with a swag of degrees and a doctorate, and considerable experience in the field of informal and radical education. And he was a jolly man, full of amusement at the world, ready to break into laughter, and always, until now, in excellent humour.

This time, however, as I walked through the door, his face fell. He spoke rapidly to a colleague, who then left. He invited me to sit down, and we engaged in a conversation that, for the first time in our relationship, was stilted and uncomfortable. After a minute or two, Jim fell silent and so did I. Time ticked on and I saw we were due at the dean's office in less that five minutes. Jim was growing visibly ill at ease.

A moment later and his colleague burst through the door, walked to the centre of the room, turned and revealed that he had a tie hanging over his forefinger. My hand went to my throat. My shirt was open at the neck. The colleague jiggled the tie a little, and Jim got up and gave it to me.

I need to explain three things. The first is that a friend of mine who had taught maths at the same university had told me that I must wear a white shirt and tie at all times, and I had tried to do this. I had. The second thing is that both my mother, when I was a child, and Marianne, when we got married, tried to get me to dress well. But neither could claim total success. And the third thing is that, before my stay in Bangkok, I had not worn a tie for years.

Red-faced, I put the tie on, and we set off at a run for the dean's office, getting there a minute, or maybe two, late. We sat in low, comfortable chairs, but other than that the meeting was conducted formally, with Jim, so to speak, in the chair. Introductions were made, cards exchanged, sentiments which I imagined both of us considered fatuous were expressed, and the meeting was over fifteen minutes later (or perhaps thirteen minutes later, so that the dean could claw back the two minutes lost because we had arrived late).

Once we were well away from the dean's office. Jim burst into laughter, his good humour restored. I made to give the tie back, but he told me to keep it. It was now the colleague's turn to look uneasy. I assume he had borrowed it from someone, or conceivably torn it from the throat of that someone, who would now have to go tieless for the rest of the day. I tried to give the tie back to the colleague later, but Jim had made it into a gift, and the colleague looked shocked at my offer.

Jim and the colleague took me to the airport the next day. We sat together and had a final coffee before I went through passport control. I was wearing my tie. Jim left us for ten minutes or so, and came back with an impossible parting gift. It was a small tray with a pen-holder and an ink well. There was no way I could put it into my carry-on bag without breaking it, so I had to go through the departure gate holding the thing in one hand and juggling my passport and bag in the other. I turned and waved my parting gift on high. They waved back, and I walked on into the departure lounge.

The pen-holder and inkwell travelled under the seat in front of me, limiting my legroom, and by the time I got to Charles de Gaulle airport, I was sick of it. I stuffed it into my cabin bag and heard it crack and break as I forced the bag closed. I went on through passport control to collect my luggage. I feel a stab of guilt as I write this, but I was on a round-the-world jaunt and had several flights to take before I got back to Sydney. I was bound to throw the thing away eventually.

And yes, I do know gifts are an important part of many cultures, and so I need to tell you that I thought I had sorted all this out when I consulted Jim a couple of days before I left. He had asked me to search out and send him good quality second-hand copies of Paulo Freire's *Pedagogy of the Oppressed* and *Pedagogy of Hope*. They would, he had told me, be my present to him.

2000s

Understanding Noah

This highlight is about suicide, and so should more properly be called a lowlight.

I believe in free will. There are people – serious thinkers – who reject free will. They argue that you may think you have made a choice to do something, but that loads of factors – like the weather, a telephone call from your brother asking you to come over and help him lift some things off a truck, a disagreement with your partner, a film you saw recently, a profound belief, and a bout of hay fever coming on – all conspire to make the choice for you. Of course this can happen, and so I had better revise my claim and say that I believe that we are capable of free will.

I agree with Rick Turner, the South African philosopher, who wrote this:

> Human beings can choose. They are not sucked into the future by stimuli to which they have to respond in specific ways. Rather human beings are continually making choices. They can stand back and look at alternatives. Theoretically they can choose about anything. They can choose whether to live or to die; they can choose celibacy or promiscuity, voluntary poverty or the pursuit of wealth, ice cream or jelly.

Turner confronts us by placing choosing to commit suicide and choosing to eat jelly in the same basket. He is saying that both can be rational acts. Again, there are people who will disagree vigorously. They will say that he is just plain wrong and that, at the moment when a person commits suicide, she or he has to be unhinged.

Noah and I worked at a university in Sydney and were involved in a peer review project that lasted some eighteen months. Over that time, we met regularly. I liked Noah. And from the way he stayed on and chatted for a short while after our meetings, I assumed that he liked me. I was in my late fifties and he was in his thirties. Occasionally, he would seek my advice, and this made me a little like a mentor to him. And very occasionally, he would call me uncle or unk. I took the chiding way he said these words as an expression of friendship.

Noah had a wicked sense of humour, and in our meetings we would laugh a lot. Noah would tell me stories about colleagues in his department that I was sure I should not repeat. Sometimes, he would rail against the bureaucracy of our organisation. And just occasionally, he dropped his easy-going façade and talked personally, so I knew his partner in life was ill.

Noah's and my paths also crossed in the course of our normal work, and I quickly learnt when his partner died. The death had been a long time coming, and Noah was resigned.

Several months later, Noah committed suicide.

I sought out Jenny, a colleague who had been a personal friend of Noah. She was sad but not distressed. Noah had organised his death carefully, she told me. He had stockpiled morphine over several months. His financial affairs were in order. On the day before he died, he had done the shopping for an elderly neighbour. Before taking the overdose, he had arranged himself neatly in bed.

Noah was a First Nations man and at his funeral, attended by some three hundred people, both black and white, there was a sense of loss but no despair. As far as anyone could see, there had been no unsoundness of mind in Noah's death, no being dragged down into some ghastly pit. After a long conversation a couple of years later, Jenny and I both felt that Noah's suicide had been the rejection of an unwanted future and a final, defiant, expression of will.

Do I have any qualms about Noah's death? Well, yes I do. In trying to deal with his death, I have to turn to another writer, this time the Brazilian philosopher-educator Paulo Freire. He wrote that 'human beings are not built in silence, but in word, in work, in action-reflection'.

We give meaning to our lives through language, through our interaction with our material and social worlds, and through reflecting on that interaction.

I do not know how I would have reacted if I had realised Noah was intent on taking his life. What do any of us do when the hypothetical flips over into reality? But I do know that I would have advised him against acting in silence.

Warned in South Africa

I was in South Africa again in 2001. I had been invited to do some teaching, first at the University of Cape Town and then at the University of Kwazulu Natal in Durban. My hosts had booked a flight for me from Cape Town to Durban, but I prevailed upon them to cash the ticket in and let me do the trip by car. It's about eighteen hundred kilometres from Cape Town to Durban and I took my time.

On the second night, I found a room in a small-town hotel and, after settling in, I wandered into the hotel bar. It was furnished and decorated to look like an English pub. There were five men there, bunched together at the end of the bar, all of them white. They stayed silent while I was served my drink, and then one of them assumed the role of inquisitor and asked me who I was, where I came from and so on. Everyone seemed happy with my first few answers – my name's Mike, Australia, I've just completed a couple of weeks' work in Cape Town.

'And where you going to now?'

'I'm on my way to Durban.'

This was greeted with indrawn breaths.

My inquisitor recovered first. 'You're not driving through the Transkei!'

Someone else said, 'My God!'

Another said, 'You'll be killed!'

My inquisitor took over again and said, 'You must drive around the Transkei.'

I remonstrated, saying that going around the Transkei would take me an extra couple of days and I didn't have the time.

'Listen to me, my friend,' my inquisitor said. 'We're trying to tell you. It is dangerous.'

'If you go,' another member of the group said, 'do the whole drive in daytime. Fill up before you go over the border. Close all the windows. Lock all the doors. Do not go off the highway. And do not stop if you run someone over.'

I drove out of the town the next morning, and on to the highway that would take me from one side of the Transkei to the other. I felt anxious, and cursed my doomsayers from the evening before. For historical reasons, the population of the Transkei is almost entirely black, and not the mix found in other parts of South Africa. Had my doomsayers been expressing a justified fear? Their reaction had seemed genuine enough. Or had they been expressing rank prejudice? No one else had said anything about the Transkei, not the people in Cape Town who rented the car to me, nor my hosts in Cape Town, nor the people who were going to be my hosts in Durban.

I relaxed as the day progressed. I saw nothing to justify the precautions the blokes in the pub told me to take. I got out of the car to stretch and walk, sometimes in open country, sometimes in towns. At one of the towns, I went into a café and chatted with some people there, like you would anywhere else in the world. I stopped and filled up at a petrol station. I picked up an elderly hitchhiker late in the afternoon to counter the soporific effects of driving all day. Maybe not what the blokes in the pub would have recommended. The hitchhiker asked me to drop him off just outside a small town, not in the main street. Perhaps he did not want to be seen with a white person. Who knows?

I ran no one over.

From the valley of a thousand hills

My time in Durban in 2001 coincided with a music festival called Awesome Africa, held on a large playing field in the Shongweni Resources Reserve. There were two stages and the crowd shifted its attention from one stage to the other as the different acts took place. The day was an eclectic mix of music and dance: African hip-hop groups, a very intellectual jazz band, a group described in the program as 'trance rockers and ravers', a kora player from Senegal, a Joni Mitchell look-and-sound-alike, a group of three men performing a powerfully rhythmic form of chant called kwaito, and the Shembes, a Christian community 'from the Valley of a Thousand Hills'.

I was with a group of people from the University of Kwazulu Natal. One of them was Pitika Ntuli, a professor of fine arts and a passionate advocate for the new South Africa.

The Shembes performed at sunset. The kora player had just finished, and there was a subdued buzz from the crowd. People were standing and stretching. Others were crowded around the food stalls. Suddenly, the air was rent by a deafening, discordant noise. On stage, four men were blowing into horns. The horns were slender, opening to small bells, and ancient-looking. One was at least two metres long. Behind the horns was the insistent beat of a drum.

A line of women, dressed in purple, came forward from the back of the stage. They were holding small shields in one hand, and staffs in the other. They danced in unison, moving very slowly, crouched side on but with their heads turned and eyes fixed on the audience. They moved forwards and backwards, and turned very slowly, every movement performed with hypnotic intensity. People fell silent. This, I thought, was a Christianity that had travelled the length of Africa, taking on African ritual and owing little to Europe or the Middle East.

The women's dance ended. They retreated and a line of men moved forward. The men, too, moved in unison, half crouched, side-on, heads turned towards the crowd, eyes intense. The men's dance seemed the same as the women's, until suddenly, with astonishing rapidity, each dancer lifted a knee high and stamped. The suddenness of the stamp, and the immediate return to slow motion, drew cries from the audience. Amidst the blare of the horns and the regular beat of the drum, the dance went on, punctuated by this stamping. I tried to anticipate the next stamp, without success, and yet always the dancers stamped in perfect unison, and the crowd responded with shouts of surprise and, because this was South Africa, high-pitched ululations.

The dance stopped. There was no climax. No formalised ending. The horns and the drum fell silent. The line of men broke up. And on stage, with a microphone in his hand, was Pitika Ntuli.

'We are truly a rainbow people,' he said. The crowd cheered. South Africans were 'a people in the making'. More cheering. By participating in the festival, the Shembes were contributing to 'the African Renaissance'. More cheering and shouting. The Shembes, the other performers, the audience in front of him were proof that together they could create a new South Africa 'based on trust and love'. The crowd cheered, clapped, danced and filled the air with ululations.

Weeping for South Africa

During my 2001 visit to South Africa, I sensed that the exhilaration I had felt in 1996 was no longer there. There were moments, of course, like the unfettered joy I witnessed at the Awesome Africa festival, but, for the most part, the mood of the country was subdued. People were settling into their roles under the post-apartheid government. The transition from extraordinary to ordinary was taking place.

In Durban, I caught up with Elena, a trade union friend. She was as busy as ever, and we only managed to meet for breakfast on my second-last day in the country. She and her partner had been critics of the apartheid regime, and had earned threats against themselves and their children. The worst was an anonymous voice on the phone late one evening telling them that 'they' were coming that night to kill all four of them.

Elena and her partner took the threat seriously. They were friends of Rick Turner, who had responded to a knock on his door one evening in 1978 and was shot dead. Elena, her partner and their children went to an upstairs room and waited out the night together. No one came.

At our breakfast, Elena asked me about the course I was working on at the university. I told her that I had made reference to the struggle against apartheid, and had been surprised when no one picked up on what I had said.

'You know,' she said, 'it is only five years since Mandela signed the new constitution, and people are already beginning to forget.'

We sat in despondent silence for a while.

'Now our poor country is facing the spread of AIDS,' Elena said.

We looked at each other.

'I don't know whether I have the energy for another struggle,' she said, and wept.

A walk in the park

My brother Sandy died several years ago at the age of seventy-four.

Sandy Newman (Anthony Newman on his birth certificate and his publications) was a scholar with an international reputation. He wrote an analysis of the work of the French novelist Nathalie Sarraute entitled *Une poesie des discours* using a combination of linguistic and literary methods. He earned the admiration of people from both disciplines, and from Sarraute herself. Sandy was writing at a time of intellectual ferment in France. Writers like Foucault, Baudrillard, Cixous, Lyotard, Kristeva and Derrida were gaining prominence and influencing thinkers across the globe. And Sandy was there, breaking new scholarly ground and doing this in another language!

I dipped into some of these people, but I came away none the wiser and fell back on those comic book versions in English – *Foucault for Beginners* and the like – in an effort to keep up.

I know this is odd after boasting about Sandy as an intellectual but I remember him best as an athlete. He was good at the long jump, and middle-distance running, but it was in rugby that he shone. He was a winger. He ran like a dream, smooth and lithe.

In 1955 and 1956, Sandy played in the first fifteen of the Sydney secondary school we both went to. He was selected for a combined schools' team, and when he went on to university he played in the Sydney first grade rugby competition. He had poor eyesight, and that prevented him from making a bid to play at state level. There was no laser surgery then.

In 1956, Sandy scored the perfect try.

The forwards were bunched to the side of the field on the halfway line, and Sandy had dropped back so that he was in the perfect position when the ball was skied. (How did he do that?) The opposition forwards bore down on him, but Sandy stood his ground, caught the ball and took off like the wind, on an angle away from the sideline towards the centre of the field. Now, both forward packs began moving towards the centre. Having set the whole field in motion, Sandy propped on one leg, changed direction and wove his way back through both packs towards the sideline.

All but the opposition's full-back were now behind him, and those of us who had seen my big brother play knew there was no contest. The full-back crouched, legs wide apart, readying himself to tackle Sandy and drive him across the sideline. Anyone else would have headed back infield and relied on speed, and Sandy did sway his body in that direction for an instant, throwing the full-back off-balance. But then, with the speed and elegance of some very fast African animal, Sandy stepped through the metre-wide gap between the full back and the sideline, sprinted and then trotted to the goal line, and touched the ball down between the posts.

Fifty-five years later, I took my brother for lunch in a pub and then for a walk in a nearby park. When the time came to drive him home and we approached the car, he made to get into the driver's seat.

'No, mate,' I said to him. 'I'm driving. You get into the passenger's seat.'

Sandy looked enquiringly at me.

'Just go round the front of the car to the other side, big brother of mine.' I indicated where he should go.

Sandy gave me an anxious smile, and walked to the front of the car. To get round to the other side, he had to step on to an asphalt path. I looked down to unlock the car door, and when I looked up, Sandy had made off along the path, walking rapidly. I called out to him, and he broke into a run. I had a wonky knee. One worked well enough after a knee replacement, but the other was still the original. I set off awkwardly after my wayward brother, shouting out his name. People looked. Sandy increased his speed. He may have been in his seventies but he was running with the ease, the fluidity, of a much younger man. The path led to a road that bordered the park and had traffic on it. Sandy was now streaking towards it (well, running faster than me; everything these days is relative), as if towards the try-line of old, and the gap between us was widening.

I lost all semblance of dignity, stopped and screamed out his name. He came to a halt, as suddenly as he had started, and stood quite still with his back to me, looking at his hands, which he held palms up front of him, seeing something no one else could see.

As I hobbled up to him, he turned and smiled a wonderful smile of surprise and pleasure. He was seeing me, his little brother, in a park, for the first time that day. He recognised me again in the long months leading up to his death, but he did not do so again with such evident joy.

Soul dancing in Hobart

In 2007, Frank, our son, was appointed artistic director of Terrapin Theatre Company based in Hobart, Tasmania. Three months after taking on the job, Frank mounted his first play in a small theatre in Hobart's harbourside district of Salamanca. Marianne and I flew from Sydney to see it.

The play mixed actors on stage and their pre-recorded images on a huge video screen. The actors could walk behind the screen and their images would continue to walk across the screen. Once on the screen, the 'actors' could fly, change shape, become tiny, and grow into giants. The actors on stage and the actors on screen interacted, sometimes in moments of intimacy and sometimes in moments of riot and pandemonium.

Terrapin had started out thirty years earlier as a puppet theatre, and its origins were honoured in a scene culminating in a dance. In the course of the story, one of the characters, a young woman, grows weak, lies down on the stage against the screen, turns on her side and dies. There is a pause, and then her soul rises out of her body. It is a pale blue, diaphanous figure, and it drifts up to the middle of the screen, where it floats, undulating slightly. It is a moment of shock at the death of the character, and then of calm and sadness.

But the moment is short-lived, because the soul explodes. The head and limbs detach from the torso, and all the parts float rapidly upwards and disappear, as if flying off the screen and into the flies of the theatre. Immediately, the separated parts of the body fall out of the flies onto the stage. They are all real objects, cushion-like, featureless, pale blue. The actor lying against the screen awakens, sits up, looks around her and sees the parts of the soul lying on the stage. She stands, gathers the parts and joins them together into a life-size puppet. Now, she hugs the puppet and the two figures circle the stage in a flowing, loving, contemplative dance.

On the way out of the theatre, a woman just behind us said, 'Wow! I didn't expect that. How amazing.'

Frank was standing a little to one side, leaning against the wall. He was dressed in a T-shirt and jeans, and looked like no one special. For a moment, I wanted to turn and say, 'That's the director over there. Go and tell him.'

But this is a highlight in which I played no part. The moment passed. Sanity prevailed. I said nothing.

A moment to remember in a Sydney clinic

As I write, both Marianne and I are in good health. However, she is in her seventies and I am in my eighties, and like many people in our age group, we have had the occasional brush with illness. Which means, of course, that we have had the occasional brush with the medical profession.

I remember sitting alongside Marianne in an oncologist's rooms in a Sydney hospital. It was our first meeting with the specialist. He had just told us that Marianne had a life-threatening disease, and he was recommending that she begin a three-month period of treatment. We were both shocked, by the news itself and by the matter-of-fact way in which the specialist talked of Marianne dying if she did not start the treatment soon, and how the treatment only had a seventy-five per cent chance of success even if she did start the treatment soon.

The specialist broke the silence. He asked Marianne if she wanted a second opinion, and said, 'I can arrange for you to see one of my colleagues.' He swivelled his chair and reached for his phone.

Marianne said, 'No, thank you.'

The specialist looked back over his shoulder.

'I do want a second opinion,' Marianne said, 'but I want it from a specialist in another hospital. Someone from this hospital would come from the same research culture as you, and we wouldn't learn anything new.'

The specialist withdrew his hand from the phone, swivelled slowly back, and looked at Marianne.

I watched him.

He was encountering Marianne for the first time.

He was recalibrating.

Our specialist wrote to a specialist in a hospital on the other side of Sydney, and we found ourselves sitting in front of the second specialist a few days later.

The second specialist read the first specialist's letter out to us, dwelling on the part of the letter in which the first specialist described Marianne as 'a very intelligent woman'. We took that as code, and that the first specialist was telling the second specialist to tread carefully.

The first specialist has proved to be excellent, humble when a treatment has not worked, genuinely pleased when the treatment has worked. We have been seeing him regularly for eighteen years now. His relationship to us has always been impeccably professional, but there is friendship as well.

At one consultation, there were three students present. Our specialist introduced them to us and asked Marianne whether she minded if they sat in.

Marianne said she had no objection, and the specialist went on, 'I was telling them before you arrived that I wanted you to have a donor stem cell transplant and that you told me to sod off.'

Marianne looked at the specialist for a moment, the slightest of smiles playing across her lips. 'I do not think,' she said, broadening her French accent a smidgen, 'that I used the word sod.'

We moved on to the business of the meeting but for the first few minutes, I could see that the specialist was having difficulty disguising his delight.

A drawing in Albi

It doesn't happen all that often, but when I really engage with a painting or drawing, it's like entering into a struggle. It's as if the painting or drawing is goading me, then rewarding me, then goading and rewarding me all over again.

I have a friend who lives near the town of Albi in the south-west of France. Guy and I worked for different community development agencies in the same area of inner London in the 1970s. He moved to France and I came home to Australia years ago. When I get to Europe these days, I try to go to Albi to see Guy and his partner Jennie. But I also go to Albi to see a drawing.

The drawing is in the permanent exhibition of paintings and drawings by Henri de Toulouse-Lautrec, which is housed in the Bishop's Palace next to the Cathedral of Saint Cécile. All those posters are there, and many of his early paintings of horses, some of his later paintings, and the occasional pen and ink drawing.

The drawing I go to see hangs in a plain frame on a good expanse of wall, so that it can be viewed alone and without the distraction of other paintings or drawings beside it. It is called *La buveuse* (the drinker), and depicts a woman, in her thirties perhaps, seated at a table with a half empty glass and a half empty bottle in front of her. From her clothes, we can see that she is working class. From the slight slouch of her body we can see she is tired. There is no hint of anyone else in the drawing, so we conclude that she is alone. We see her in profile. Her chin is propped in her left hand. And her gaze…well, that's it. Toulouse-Lautrec has captured the moment when the drink kicks in and when the gaze shifts inwards.

I stand and I look. How can the artist have caught that instant?

How, with a few strokes of a pen, can he show the woman's pain: her cynicism slipping into distraction?

I want the woman in the drawing to turn and look towards me, but of course she does not, and so the drawing goads me. Her right arm lies across the table in front of her, and I notice her other hand hanging idly over the table's edge, lost in the shadow, limp, capturing the woman's mood – beautiful, terrible – and the drawing rewards me.

2010s

Enlightenment at Saint-Benoît-sur-Loire

I like to think that I had my belief system (or, more accurately, my non-belief system) challenged in 2018. I was racing towards eighty and it seemed an appropriate age for this to happen. I was accompanying Marianne, who was on retreat at Saint-Benoît-sur-Loire, one of the oldest abbeys of the Benedictine rule, situated, as its name says, close to the river Loire, and dating from the eleventh century.

We were provided with full bed and board in an annex to the monastery, and attended various services (offices, they call them in French) in the monastery chapel. These were conducted six times a day by some forty monks who flickered about in long black robes, looking benign when their hoods were down, and sinister when their hoods were up. All the offices were sung, in a kind of substandard Gregorian chant that I found comfortably soporific. Marianne attended most of the offices every day, and I attended one or two. For the rest of the day, I walked along the banks of the Loire, sat in the café of the village huddled under the walls of the monastery, or lay on the bed in our room in the annex and read.

A couple of days into the retreat, I was at a late morning office, sitting by myself well back from the chancel where the monks were doing their business, and from the first few pews of the nave where Marianne and a scatter of others taking time out at the monastery were doing theirs. I was relaxed after a long walk, and that may have made me susceptible to the stark beauty of the medieval chapel with its soaring walls, its windows set high up in those walls, and its precise and elegant stonework. I was speculating on the life and times of the long-dead stonemasons responsible for all this when I became aware that I had been picked out by a shaft of light.

Now, as I have already told you, I am a secular soul, but for a thrilling moment I thought, well, this has got to be what they are talking about, the finger pointing down, and a voice saying, 'You there, yes you. Newman, isn't it? What's all this about you not believing in Me?' I looked around. No one else in the chapel, layperson or monk, was similarly lit up. Had I been chosen? But disappointments come thick and fast in this little life of ours. I looked up, the light shining on my upturned face, and saw that the divine spotlight was sunlight reflecting off a window high up in the right-hand transept of the chapel and shining down through one of the windows in the nave. What is more, the shaft of light had already shifted and was lighting up the empty place beside me. I watched as it continued its move along the empty pew towards the central aisle, where it faded to nothing, and in that moment I abandoned my momentary temptation to take a Pascalian punt and I turned my thoughts to lunch.

Those of us staying at Saint-Benoît-sur-Loire ate well. What is more, there was a bottle of very drinkable *vin de table* thrown in for both lunch and dinner. Although she is French, Marianne sometimes discourages me from drinking at lunchtime, and that means that if I do have a glass, it is done with a slight sense of guilt. But there was no tormented conscience at Saint-Benoît. If the monks reckon it is all right to drink at lunchtime, then it must be.

Cross-cultural miscommunication in le Périgord

When Marianne and I married in 1968, I was the first foreigner to join my extended French family. Susan, the Scot, was the next. She married one of our nephews in 1983. Then there was Hannah, who married another of our nephews. She was German. (She divorced her way out of the family in the late 1980s.) Monique, our niece, formed a longstanding relationship with Frederik who is Finnish and Belgian. And for a while, a Portuguese looked as if she might join us, but she got cold feet at the last moment and fled to New York.

There were reasons for this kind of mixing and matching. In the 1970s and 1980s, there was a huge amount of travel going on all over the developed world, and particularly in Europe. Young people moved easily among EU countries, working for a while and then moving on again. In 1987, a program called Erasmus was established. This allowed university students to complete part of their studies at a university in another European country.

Marianne and I were driving from the south to Paris in 1992, and we called in on Janos, a Hungarian artist we knew. He and his partner Zoe, who was also Hungarian, lived in Vacqueras, near Orange. Around the table that evening were Janos and Zoe, three Germans, a Spaniard, and Marianne and me. The conversation was fast and furious and in all the languages represented at the table. If any of the party was having trouble understanding, then whoever had the right language or languages stepped in as an impromptu interpreter. There was a lot of laughter, and a sense of delight at how we were making the evening work.

Laetitia's youngest son is Dominic, and he met Wei-Tao, who is Taiwanese, in 2001. They are both musicians and were working and studying in Paris. In 2006, they married in Taipei, then returned to France, where Laetitia organised a second 'wedding' in le Périgord, a central region of France.

The event took place in an abandoned hamlet, which had been turned into a function centre. The centre looked agreeably down-at-heel but had everything necessary for the festivities, which consisted of a pre-wedding lunch on Friday, the event proper on Saturday evening, and then a post-wedding brunch on Sunday. Some sixty people were invited, and Laetitia managed to lodge them all in a variety of forms of accommodation in the surrounding towns and villages.

Laetitia and her partner Eric had gone to Taipei for the Taiwanese wedding, and a delegation of Taiwanese came to France for the French wedding. The delegation was made up of Wei-Tao's mother and father, her sister, and her aunt and uncle. Eric had been charged with looking after the Taiwanese delegation for two days in Paris and then to get them to le Périgord by train. The Taiwanese had no French and no English (not that Eric's English was much chop anyway). I was at the function centre on the Thursday when Eric and the Taiwanese delegation arrived. Both parties looked pretty frazzled.

Eric had continued to look after the Taiwanese delegation for the Thursday evening and then conducted them to the pre-wedding lunch, which took place on a terrace, overlooking an open field and then a wood. Eric looked even more stressed, and I joined him and the Taiwanese, intending to give him a break. I will admit that I only did so because I saw that Wei-Tao was with them and could act as interpreter.

I gave Eric the nod and he departed with inelegant haste. I turned to the delegation. Wei-Tao introduced me. There followed a period in Mandarin, but because they kept looking at me, I assumed it was a question and answer session about who I was exactly, and what was an Australian doing there anyway. We were called to the tables on the terrace, and so I contributed little to the conversation. However, before we sat down, I asked Wei-Tao to translate something I wanted to say to her uncle. The three of us stood to one side, with the uncle looking at me expectantly.

I said (in French) to Wei-Tao, 'Tell your uncle that he and I are the same. We are both your uncles.'

Wei-Tao translated, but she was interrupted by Laetitia calling us laggards to the table. Wei-Tao continued her translation but the uncle was not listening. He was looking at me with extraordinary pleasure. He grabbed my hand and shook it enthusiastically, speaking all the while. I looked around for help from Wei-Tao, but Laetitia was in the process of seating her next to Dominic at the top of the main table. The uncle continued talking to me. I had thought that the fact that a Taiwanese and an Australian were both Wei-Tao's uncles was amusing, but had not thought it would do more than elicit a smile. I had only said it because I had liked the look of the uncle, and wanted to establish some kind of rapport with him. I took my place at the table for lunch in a mildly troubled state of mind.

Over the next two days, I sought the uncle out and then he sought me out, and we tried to communicate, but with no real success. I had hoped that Wei-Tao would be nearby on one of these occasions to help us clarify what was going on, but that did not happen. Not unreasonably, she was taken up with the business of being the bride.

The wedding was a success. Once again, I felt as if I was in a French film. All the eating was outdoors. The major dinner on Saturday was under three beautiful oak trees in the field below the abandoned village. Dominic's sister and three brothers all gathered on a stage with a huge red paper screen illuminated from behind and acting as a backdrop. They all spoke lovingly of their youngest brother and of Wei-Tao. After dinner, we climbed to the highest point of the hamlet, where we lit candles inside paper spheres and set the spheres floating into the night sky, to fall we knew not where.

The scene was beautiful, but for an Australian, it was also profoundly distressing. It was midsummer and I had images of the things lodging in the eaves of houses in nearby villages or setting a grass fire raging across the land destroying all flora and fauna in its path, but no one else seemed the slightest bit concerned. So when in Rome... Marianne and I lit a candle and sent our sphere floating gently up and away on its mission of destruction.

Some thirty of us gathered the next morning for a final brunch. I half expected the police to be there to take us all into custody for destroying several villages, setting fire to valuable crops and immolating the odd farmer, but nothing like that eventuated.

I had sought out Wei-Tao, and asked her to see if she, her uncle and I could get together and clarify matters, whatever those matters were. Wei-Tao wandered off and was taken aside by some one else, so it was after lunch, when we were all listening to the children at the event performing a concert of various kinds of music, that she got back to me. She led me on to the terrace where we had the first lunch. The explanation was simple. Her uncle held a senior post in the Taipei police. When I said that we were both the same, he thought I was saying that I was a policeman too.

When we were saying goodbye a couple of hours later, Wei-Tao's uncle and I looked at each other ruefully. I smiled and made a gesture intended to express regret. He did the same. It may have been a bit late in the day, but it was a perfect moment of cross-cultural communication.

Drag night in Honolulu

I was invited to a conference to be held in Manhattan (comma, sigh of disappointment) Kansas in May 2015, and accepted. The travel agent I consulted offered me flights from Sydney to Denver and then on to Manhattan (Kansas). The flight to Denver was over fifteen hours, and so I asked the agent to organise a one-night stopover in Honolulu each way, and to book me into an airport hotel.

By and large, the travelling went well. I got there, and I got back. But my so-called 'airport hotel' in Honolulu was not quite what I expected. It was in a run-down industrial estate just outside the airport boundaries, was made of red brick, and had those open walkways along the side of the building that you find on British public housing estates. The hotel did not have too many amenities but it did have a bar, and I dropped in on my first stay there to find it occupied by about ten very large Hawaiians who were in the middle of a karaoke night.

There was a man with a short black beard standing alone at the end of the bar, from where he could survey the whole room and see everyone who came and went through the bar room door to his right. He was clearly the gatekeeper. Bars have different cultures, and going into one you do not know can require certain courtesies. I made a point of saying hello to the gatekeeper, and he looked me up and down, apparently approved of what he saw, and told me to help myself to the food that was in large trays on a table against the wall.

'Are you sure that's OK?' I asked him.

'If anyone says it isn't, they'll have to answer to me,' he said, and I relaxed. I had a protector.

I helped myself to some food, drank a glass of wine, and headed to bed. I did not sing.

I dropped into the bar some eight days later on my way back to Australia. My flight had landed well into the evening and it was after ten when I pushed the bar door open. This time, there were thirty or forty people present and the joint was jumping. The gatekeeper was there, same position, same presence. He looked at me quizzically, and I reminded him that I had been there a week before. He nodded, said we were celebrating the birthdays of three people, and told me to help myself to some food, which I did.

I got a drink, turned away from the bar, and stood there for a moment with a plate in one hand and a glass in the other. The people at a table nearby invited me to join them and, once I had settled in, one of them said, 'You're just in time.'

'What for?'

'The drag show.'

There was a pub near our house in Sydney, now sadly gone, that had drag shows, and I had caught sight of splendid people strutting their stuff on the bar as I walked by. And gay friends of ours celebrated twenty years of their relationship by holding a party in their house, to which they invited three extravagantly dressed drag queens to perform a floorshow. From this limited experience, I am prepared to say that Sydney drag queens are slender – usually tall, sometimes masculine looking, but always slender.

The three drag queens (do drag queens always come in threes?) who performed in the bar of this down-at-heel Honolulu hotel were enormous! Giants. The size of second row forwards in a national rugby team. And the evening was suitably gigantic and riotous. The noise tripled as people shouted, cheered and laughed, and the drag queens bumped and ground, mimed, sang, and danced and danced and danced. One had a skirt split to the waist, and the thigh on display was huge and surprisingly pale. Each time the thigh was displayed, the crowd roared.

Somehow, my glass was refilled, and refilled, and I settled in for the evening. And I am glad that I did. When the show was over, the three drag queens moved through the crowd chatting to people they knew and, in my case, someone they did not know. I spoke to all three. From my limited experience, I would say that Sydney drag queens can be as in-your-face offstage as on. Not so in Honolulu. Each of these giant Hawaiians was softly spoken, self-effacing and touchingly demure.

I got on to my plane for the flight to Sydney the next morning. I had a headache, but it was a small price to pay.

PS: A drag show crosses boundaries. It is an escape from convention. The crowd is like a bunch of kids let off a bus at a beach after being cooped up for a couple of hours. They run wild.

On that evening in Honolulu, one of the drag queens had a fan. 'She' flicked it open, held it just below two heavily made-up eyes, and suddenly showed some leg. Why wouldn't the crowd roar?

An old flame in a moral philosophy class in Sydney

I tried my hand at a number of jobs in my twenties, but from my early thirties until my retirement, I worked in the field of adult education. For some thirty years, I was a teacher or organiser or administrator or researcher and writer, and it was only in retirement that I enjoyed adult education as a student.

I had an agreeable experience in a moral philosophy class, held at the Sydney Workers' Educational Association, in February 2020. Our group of about fifteen was already assembled in the classroom when the tutor entered, accompanied by a slender woman. He announced that the woman would be joining us for just that morning, to make up for a session she had missed in a class he taught on another day.

There was a place vacant next to me, and the woman sat down. We looked at each other with interest, because we had spent time together in the early 1960s. We had kicked around London, seen films and shows together, drunk in pubs and done some hitchhiking, all the way to Paris on one occasion. We had drifted apart after a few months and that was that. I think she may have headed for Turkey.

Our paths had crossed in the very early 1990s but that encounter was not a success. I had not recognised her straight away and when I did and we talked, I could see that she was mightily irritated. I managed to tell her that I had stayed in the UK for seventeen years or so after we split up, and she managed to tell me that she had stayed in Italy then the USA. We learnt enough about each other's circumstances to be able to make contact again, but neither of us did.

Now, here we were, catching up on the past twenty-seven years during a pair-work exercise in a philosophy class. I leant in close and felt the warmth of her body on my cheek. She tilted her head and looked down, stretching her neck ever so slightly. Now she looked up at me. How, oh how, had I forgotten those eyes?

I glanced up and saw our teacher watching us with interest. He had recently arrived from Denmark, and may have wondered whether it was normal in Australia for two people, who had only just met, to work together with such evident pleasure over a passage from Kierkegaard (on commitment).

As luck would have it, that morning was my turn to give a ten-minute presentation. There was some kind of irony in the fact that I had chosen to talk about David Rieff's book *In praise of forgetting*. I walked out to the front of the classroom, and performed before my girlfriend of yesteryear. She sat back with a conniving smile on her face. I had lost some weight over the previous year and I turned and wrote on the whiteboard a little more often that I might otherwise have done.

I had to leave the class before the end to get to an appointment. I asked her just before I slipped away if she would be coming to the class again and she said no.

She said something like, 'So that will be that.'

We smiled. I shrugged. She shrugged. I was standing, and she was sitting. I let my hand touch her shoulder. She did not flinch. I left.

I did not try to contact her and I knew she would not try to contact me. The moment, though, had been great fun, and a bit like the time I was crossing a road here in Sydney, and a person crossing the road in the opposite direction patted me on my (ever so slight) pot belly and said, 'I have one of those.' I had been at university with him – we had worked together on *Honi Soit*, the student newspaper – but that was more than forty years ago and I had not seen him since. Neither of us stopped. It was too perfect an encounter to spoil with a tedious chat in which we might discover that we had nothing in common.

Finding the right word in a Sydney pub, and other fragments

There was a period early on in the progress of my brother's Alzheimer's when he was conscious of his condition and we could talk about it. I remember sitting in his kitchen. His partner Margaret was washing up a couple of bowls that were too big for the dishwasher. Sandy was standing close to her and so she handed him a tea towel.

Sandy accepted it, and looked around at me with a disarming smile. 'I'm not sure what I do with this,' he said. Confusion, awareness, self-deprecation, all mixed together.

A major symptom of Sandy's illness was an inexorable loss of language. In the early days, he made his frustration obvious by cursing or groaning when he lost his way in a sentence or could not find the word he wanted. These lapses increased in frequency until every attempt at conversation became a failure.

For a while, I took Sandy to lunch in a pub I liked, and it was at one such lunch that Sandy let fly with a string of quiet, impeccably pronounced expletives.

'Bugger this thing I've got. Fuck. This bloody…this bloody…' Sandy fumbled in his jacket pocket and brought out a small notebook, opened it, flicked over the pages and then looked up and said, 'This bloody Alzheimer's!'

I sat looking at him. He looked at me.

He waved his notebook in the air, and then slipped it gloriously back into his pocket. 'Fuck,' he said, 'Alzheimer's, Alzheimer's, Alzheimer's.'

I rang at ten one morning. A man whose voice I did not recognise answered. Margaret had gone out, he said. He was a carer. I told him who I was.

'Your brother is still sleeping,' he said.

'I'll ring back later,' I said and hung up.

The brief conversation set me wondering, 'Does Sandy still dream? And when he wakes, does he know that he is no longer dreaming?'

A few days later, I went to collect Sandy for one of our lunches. The husk of my brother was present, bent slightly forward, looking at his hands, which he held waist-high in front of him, with both palms up. My big brother was past the stage when he might have helped me answer any of my footling questions about dreams.

In our waking lives, we are constrained by a whole raft of rules and regulations, and those unremarkable routines we have developed in order to get through the day. To manage, and to live in reasonable safety, we have to be sensible in our actions and civil in our words. But then, at the end of our sensible and civil day, we go to bed and we sleep, and we dream, and we take leave of our senses. We step outside time, defy the laws of physics, escape the limitations of rational thought, and enter a realm of chaotic meaninglessness. We go mad.

Sandy did any number of odd things, like putting the post in the washing basket, and turning chairs to face the wall. And while he could still speak, he would ask about that other person moving about the house, although there was no one there. At least there was no one there when I went to look. This set me thinking of my lost mate Brian, and I imagined him leaning against the window of his Oxford Street frock shop, and quietly intoning another passage by T.S. Eliot, this time from the *Wasteland*:

> Who is the third who walks always beside you?
> When I count, there are only you and I together
> But when I look ahead up the white road
> There is always another one walking beside you
> Gliding wrapt in a brown mantle, hooded
> I do not know whether a man or a woman…

Sandy may have been respected in the fields of French language and literature, but his other passion was music. While completing his doctorate at the university of Besançon, in the east of France, he founded a choir, which continued to flourish long after he left. And when he returned to Sydney, he founded a semi-professional choir, which has been an established part of the music scene in Sydney for the past forty years.

I loved the way Sandy conducted. His gestures were restrained at the beginning of each piece of music but little by little they would become more urgent. He would hold out both arms and lean forward as if drawing the music out of each singer. And when the choir was in full voice, he would raise his arms and mark out huge rhythmic circles in the air.

One time. we got home early from the pub. I looked through Sandy's collection of CDs and played him some of his favourite music – Purcell, Byrd, Dvorak (not for me!), Bach – but I got little or no reaction. I sang a round to him that he and I used to sing at student parties all those years ago,

> There goes the happy moron
> He doesn't give a damn
> I wish I were a moron
> By God, perhaps I am!

And the Ben Johnson drinking song,

> Drink today, and drown all sorrow
> You shall perhaps not do it tomorrow
> Best, while you have it, use your breath
> There is no drinking after death.

Sandy remained unmoved.

There was a period when Sandy spoke a lot but what he said made no sense. Some of the words were recognisable, and some of the recognisable words suggested a life of erudition, but they bore no relation one to the other. Each hung in the air on its own, bereft of meaning. 'assiduous'. Or perhaps it was the adverb, 'assiduously'.

Near the end, when Sandy was bedridden, I clung to images of him as an athlete. I was telling my friend Peter Willis about Sandy's prowess at rugby, and I described Sandy scoring the perfect try.

Peter had lived for a long time in close contact with an Indigenous community in the Kimberley. He pointed out that I was probably the only person who remembered the try, and then he said, 'In that respect, you are the keeper of your brother's spirit.'

'Sandy has died.'

I received the news and sat there. And then I asked myself, 'So what was the point? What was the point of Sandy's perfect try? What was the point of his choirs? What was the point of his intellectually elegant book (written in French) on the novels of Nathalie Sarraute?

I have argued that our dreams are meaningless. Maybe our waking lives are meaningless too. Perhaps the Bard was right. In *The Tempest*, Ariel assumes the form of a harpy, conjures up a magical banquet attended by spirits and phantoms, and then, with a clap of her harpy wings, dismisses them. To the 'real' people left on stage, Prospero says,

> ... These our actors,
> As I foretold you, were all spirits and
> Are melted into air, into thin air:
> And, like the baseless fabric of this vision,
> The cloud-capp'd towers, the gorgeous palaces,
> The solemn temples, the great globe itself,
> Yea, all which it inherit, shall dissolve
> And, like this insubstantial pageant faded,
> Leave not a rack behind. We are such stuff
> As dreams are made on, and our little life
> Is rounded with a sleep...

Albert Camus, the French philosopher, thinks there is no point. There is no god, no set of absolute principles, no reason for being, and yet we live out our lives as if there were. Absurd though it is, we will spend our lives giving purpose to a purposeless existence.

At first glance, Camus' concept of the absurd seems defeatist. If there is no point, then why get out of bed? But the opposite is the case. With Camus' absurd comes an exhilarating freedom. If there is no one there to give us meaning, then we will have to make that meaning ourselves. The world is our oyster. In Camus' 'hopeless encounter between human questioning and the silence of the universe', the onus falls back on us to create our own reason for being.

The musings of a doting grandfather

I want to write about Frank's and Claudia's daughters Sienna and Vivi (Vivienne). At the time of this highlight, Sienna was nine, and Vivi was four. But to explain the daughters I need to describe their mother.

Claudia is an artist. Her full professional name is Claudia Damichi. She paints murals and canvases. The murals are giant patterns. They confront you. The paintings depict the real and the surreal, and challenge the viewer with their unexpected juxtaposition of colours.

Many of Claudia's paintings depict interiors, furnished with chairs. The chairs have light frames and are piled on top of each other, or tilted against each other, or lying on their sides. They cast shadows, and most of those shadows will be meticulously accurate. But when one looks closely, some part of the shadow may be intriguingly 'wrong'.

For a period, Claudia included exotic, brightly coloured birds in her interiors. These birds were inventions. The chair on which the bird was perched cast a shadow but the bird did not.

In some of the interiors, colours play the more important role. So Claudia depicts a lamp on a table against a wall. The wall has a pattern of strong colours. The lampshade has a small, denser pattern of equally strong colours that clash with those of the wall.

Marianne and I pick our granddaughters up from school once a week and spend the rest of the afternoon with them. We do different things, but end up at our house, where the girls paint. Normally, we alternate, picking Vivi up one week and Sienna the next, but there are times when we have them both.

The girls sit on either side of our kitchen table, facing but not looking at each other. Both of them paint with a flourish, using firm lines and starkly contrasting colours. I watch them, entranced.

Sienna has fair hair and a fair complexion (like me) and Vivi has dark hair and an olive-skinned complexion (like Marianne). They present a picture of contrasting colours, like their paintings, and their mother's paintings. I smile at the thought. But then, these are the inconsequential musings of a doting grandfather.

Time well spent with a friend in Sydney

I am at an age when it is increasingly normal to lose friends. Of course there is a mildly worrying corollary, which is that I might not lose them, they might lose me.

This is about David Spode, my antiquarian bookseller mate. David died several years ago. I had counted him as a close friend, although months could pass without either of us contacting the other.

David and I shared two adventures of Homeric proportions.

The first was in 1963, when three of us – the other person was Mungo MacCallum – loaded that car onto a ship in Sydney, offloaded it in Colombo, and drove to Athens. This is not the time for further details about the trip but simply to celebrate the fact that David's and my friendship survived several months on terrible roads in the uncomfortable confines of a clapped out Morris 1000…

The second of these epic adventures with David took place in Sydney in 2006.

David, Alan Walker (another old, old friend) and I met up at noon in Taylor's Square, Sydney, and made our way to a pub on Crown Street. There we enjoyed one of the long and bibulous lunches the three of us occasionally had together. Well into the afternoon, we walked back up Crown Street, and David suggested we finish the lunch off with another bottle of wine at his place. Alan opted out, I opted in, and David and I walked the short distance to his house, which was hidden away in a small back lane of the inner-city suburb of Surry Hills.

David operated his antiquarian book business from home. His small house was on two levels. The ground floor was filled with shelf upon shelf of books, except for a small workshop in one corner, where he restored damaged books with infinite care. David had turned the upstairs level into his apartment, and there the walls, including the walls of the stairwell, were festooned with paintings, drawings, prints and hangings, which he had collected throughout his life.

Two of the drawings were from the late Mughal period in India, and I had been with David when he bought them from an elderly man in Agra. The man had invited us into his house, offered us tea, and then, with great courtesy and, I believe, some amusement, let David haggle over the price.

The hangings and the rugs draped across a large sofa in David's apartment were all in rich and warm colours, and the whole effect was of a comfortable cocoon in which one could relax and reflect. David and I settled into his cocoon, and we drank and we talked. We talked politics, which we always did for a while. Then we talked about common friends, particularly from our time in London, which we always did for a little while longer.

The wine was good, we were comfortable, and, as the afternoon drifted into evening, we found ourselves reviewing our friendship. We talked about meeting for the first time, in 1958 in Wesley College at the University of Sydney, and about working in student theatre. David was a gifted set designer and director. We talked about that trip through Sri Lanka, India, Pakistan, Iran, Turkey and into Greece. We talked about our respective marriages, his in London, mine in Paris. We talked about David's divorce and his coming out. And we talked about coming back to Sydney, David in the mid 1970s, me, along with Marianne and the kids, in the early 1980s.

Somewhere around nine in the evening, with the conversation unfinished, we went to a restaurant in Oxford Street, and ate, and drank, and talked some more. It was one of those times when the magic happens, when the mood is right, when the company is entirely amiable, when the conversation is honest and good, and when all becomes well with the world.

I walked home about midnight, not sober, no, but not drunk either, just pleased to have spent time with a friend.

Chaos in Coledale

Alicia, our circus performer daughter, was in the final weeks of rehearsal for a show being staged in Sydney. She, her partner Hall, and their two children Gus, aged six, and Maya, aged four, lived in Coledale, a former coal-mining village on the coast, some eighty kilometres south of Sydney. Alicia had to commute to Sydney each day, and she asked Marianne and me to take over child-minding duties for the fortnight before the show opened. We agreed.

Hall worked as a production manager at the Sydney Opera House, and left early and got home late. This meant that Marianne and I had to find accommodation nearby and turn up at Alicia's house at seven a.m., take the kids to school and preschool at nine, pick them up at three p.m., and occupy them until one or other of their parents got home. All went well for the first two days, and then Marianne went down with flu. Suddenly I was looking after two energetic and demanding kids on my own.

Two days into my stint of sole grandparenting, I picked up the kids in the afternoon from school and preschool, and drove them to their house. We went in, sat down and looked at each other.

'All right,' I said. 'Let's decide what we're going to do.'

'Can we watch television?'

'You know that's not on. Your mum and dad said no television.'

'Aw,' they said. (I had, of course, thought to myself that I would use television as a last resort, but I was not yet at my wits' end.)

'We could play a game.'

There were some board games, which Gus could play and Maya could cause confusion trying to play. We had had a lot of fun yesterday. But that was yesterday. I went on…

'Or I could take you to the playground at Thirroul.'

The kids perked up. Thirroul is a town a few kilometres further south, with a park backing on to the beach, and a superbly equipped playground with all kinds of climbing frames, a flying fox and loads of swings.

'It's your choice.'

Gus and Maya looked at each other. 'Let's go to the playground,' they both said. A clear majority. No need for a recount.

We got back into the car and drove to Thirroul. I parked in a space next to the children's playground and got out. Gus got out on my side of the car and stood next to me. Maya got out on the other side, raced towards the line of swings and threw herself forward so that her tummy hit the seat of the swing. The swing wobbled wildly, and Maya slid forward and dived nose first into the ground. The ground was that rubbery stuff they use in places where kids play, and in pavements outside pubs, and Maya bounced a bit. Gus and I thought the whole thing was funny and we stood there laughing.

The playground was busy, and young parents looked at us from where they were guiding their children along small elevated walkways, or standing near their children on the climbing frames so as to catch them if they fell, and being loving, protective and caring. What they saw was Gus and me laughing at a little child's distress. Maya shrieked and I walked to her and lifted her up. Blood was streaming from her nose, all down her front and mine. I know that you are meant to hold the head forward and down to stem a nosebleed, but some misplaced instinct overrode this knowledge and made me hold her face upwards across my chest so that she gurgled and splattered blood and nasal muck about.

Disapproving young parents looked on as I took Maya back to the car and laid her down, still face upwards, on the back seat. I stood there, now very much in the public eye. All I wanted was to get Maya home, and so I looked around for Gus, but he was nowhere to be seen. I stared across the top of the car at the playground, suppressing the rising panic.

There were lots of awful young parents but no Gus. Then I saw him. He was more than a hundred metres away, watching a group of older kids kick a soccer ball around. How had he got there so quickly? Driven by embarrassment at his grandfather's ineptitude, I imagine.

I told Maya that I was going to fetch Gus.

'Not fetch,' she said. 'Get.'

'Jesus.'

I walked across the children's playground, amidst a general attitude of opprobrium. When Gus was within hearing distance, I shouted his name and he must have heard the rising anger in my voice, because he came running.

I got both of them to sit up in the back of the car and strapped them in. Maya was bleeding less, and in a sullen mood, probably because we had laughed at her.

Gus was silent for a moment or two as I drove away from the playground, but then he spoke, using my grandparently moniker of 'Mich', which is pronounced 'Meesh' and is short for Michel, which is the French equivalent of Michael. 'Mich,' he said, 'that was a bad decision.'

I pulled over to the side of the road, and unstrapped myself so that I could turn completely to look at my grandson. My union past took over, and I said, 'Gus, the decision to come to the playground was made in committee.'

I knew that Maya and Gus would not have understood what I had just said, but they remained silent, and my distress dissipated as I drove away from the playground.

When a meeting goes into committee, the participants abandon formal meeting procedure and throw the matter open to general discussion. This is called 'a committee of the whole', and its purpose is to relax the limits of formal meeting procedure and allow for a more open exchange of views.

'You okay with that, Gus?' I called over my shoulder.

The dark art of labelling

I am eighty-one years old. And I have just been told that I have dementia.

How did this awful state of affairs come about? I do not mean the dementia itself, but the declaration that I have it. I am talking about a health professional looking me in the eyes and announcing, 'You have dementia.'

Getting the language right has its pitfalls. How, for example, do I tell my friends? Do I say 'I am demented?' Or do I say, 'I have dementia?'

'I am demented' sounds as if I burst out of my flat and into the street every midnight and roar and howl and snarl and eat bits off my next-door neighbour's privet hedge. 'I have dementia,' sounds well-mannered, and suitably apologetic.

Actually, I think I will give both phrases a miss. And I won't tell my friends because, if I do, each time I see any of them, they will watch me uneasily for signs that the deplorable deterioration is kicking in.

I belong to a group whose lunch-time meetings are run on red wine and rapid-fire chiacking. Just imagine the humiliation when they begin making allowances for me. Just imagine the humiliation when they laugh sympathetically at something I say that is not remotely funny! Just imagine the humiliation when the most solicitous amongst them tries to stop me having a second glass! 'Mike, mate, are you really sure you should…?'

No, I shall say nothing to anyone except my partner Marianne because, even with the best will in the world, everyone else will define me in terms of this disease, and not in terms of my character or the things I have done in this world, like captaining my school's second grade cricket team in 1957.

But to the matter in hand… I had been depressed, not clinically depressed, but down in the mouth, and Marianne wanted me to get some counselling. I had resisted, but agreed when she suggested we go to our GP and ask her to mediate.

At the meeting with the GP, Marianne argued her case, I argued mine, and neither of us gave an inch.

Faced with the prospect of a failed meeting, our GP said, 'I know! Why don't I give you a referral to a gerontologist! They can talk over how you're feeling, what kind of exercise you might take up, what kind of medication might help, what you might read, and what kinds of support group exist.'

Reluctantly, I agreed and, ten days later, Marianne and I found ourselves waiting to see a gerontologist (and a student doctor, who I had agreed could sit in on the consultation). If I look back now, I can see that the selection of the gerontologist was done on the run and without much thought. Our GP got his name and details from a list provided on line by the Gray Lakes Medical Facility – hospital to you and me. Our GP did not know him, and Marianne and I did not google him. Not unnaturally all three of us assumed that, in this struggle called Life, he would be on our side.

I quickly formed a dislike for the man. He had a mane of black hair, which he tossed back from time to time, and a surprisingly low voice that may or may not have been cultivated. And as he led us to his room, did I see him give a little hoppity-skippity of joy, as in 'Boy oh boy, I think I've got one here!'

The gerontologist asked me to talk about my life.

'What. All of it?' I said.

'All of it,' he said, but he had lost interest by the time I reached 1943 (and the British navy) and we moved on to a test. This comprised a number of oral questions, some poorly drawn puzzles on a single sheet of paper, and some simple arithmetic. He did not say what the test was meant to achieve.

The gerontologist started with the question, 'What day is it?'

Marianne and I looked at each other, incredulous. This question has been discredited for years. Retired people have no reason to keep a check on the date in the way working people do. For us, days elide. We lose track. The company I keep at the local pub is much the same no matter what day it is.

But the fates were on my side. I had consulted my phone on arriving at the hospital and I knew the answer. But as often as not I don't.

And the 'What day is it?' question reminded me of June, a colleague and friend from yesteryear:

On a Friday evening, after eating a meal with her partner Peter, June felt a strong headache coming on. As the evening progressed, the headache got worse until Peter called an ambulance, which took June to hospital, where she quickly sank into a coma.

On Saturday morning, June woke briefly and a youngish doctor leaned over her bed and said, 'Hello, June. I am your doctor. Can you tell me what day it is?'

To which June said, 'What kind of stupid fucking question is that!' And died.

I have often wondered what happened to that young doctor. Did he stay in medicine, or did he move into another trade altogether? Policeman? Barista? Jeweller? Travelling drug salesman? What would you have done?

Back to our troubling encounter with the gerontologist…

I made an attempt to tell him about June but failed. He moved on to his next question, which was, 'Do you know where you are?'

All right, but what did he mean by where? His surgery? The Gray Lakes Medical Thingummy? The suburb? The city? On the road to extinction as a species?

There were other questions but I forget what they were or how I answered them. June floated in the reaches of the room, smiling and wanting to talk. This is something I do from time to time. I say the name of a friend who has died and I have a murmured conversation with them. Sydney is a big enough city for this kind of behaviour in public places to go unremarked. The person I speak with the most is my dad, and our discussion becomes a kind of debate in which I try to understand his pacifism.

Back to the test. Things were not going well. The gerontologist was taking his test seriously and my asides were unwelcome. Now he produced a sheet of paper with various images on it. I remember two of them – an incomplete 3D outline of a box, unintentionally (I presume) resembling a coffin, and a clock with no hands! I kid you not. A clock with no hands!

Sweat broke out on the palms of my hands and I got a lot of this part of the test wrong.

I did wonder whether the gerontologist understood the terrible symbolism of the coffin and the clock with no hands. 'No time left for you, my friend! Just finish your salmon mousse and climb into this box thing. Death's old banger is waiting outside with the motor running.' The gerontologist asked me to draw in the hands for four-thirty on the clock face, but by now I had that immortal passage from the *Rubaiyat* of Omar Khayyam ringing quietly in my ears:

> The Moving Finger writes; and, having writ,
> Moves on: nor all thy Piety nor Wit
> Shall lure it back to cancel half a Line,
> Nor all thy Tears wash out a Word of it.

I wanted to recite it to the gerontologist, but he wanted to get on with the test. I put the little hand at four and the big hand at… Ah bugger this. It was a long time since I had watched *Playschool*. And my last couple of wristwatches had digital faces anyway.

Next came a test of my numeracy skills. The gerontologist asked me to count backwards from a hundred by sevens: so 100 minus 7 is 93; 93 minus 7 is 86 (maybe)… This is, of course, what we retired people are constantly doing. You can see us in doctors' waiting rooms all over the country, mumbling to ourselves, fearful that if we get the simple arithmetic wrong, the medical system will send us off to a home, and distant cousins, waving powers of attorney, will begin circling.

Again, I tried to get the gerontologist's attention, this time to explain that I had no real schooling until we returned to Australia from the islands in 1948. I had never mastered my times tables, and my spelling is atrocious.

In view of this, I wanted to express my doubts about the suitability of the test, but the gerontologist held his hand up to silence me. And then, scribbling in the margin of that piece of paper of his, he calculated the total I had scored. I waited. He looked up and said I had scored 18 out of 32.

A pass, folks, a palpable pass! More than fifty per cent! Yeah!

The gerontologist spoke across me to his student, and then pronounced that I had dementia. I asked him to repeat himself, and he said I had dementia. Then, abruptly, he left the room. The student, Marianne and I waited. Was the gerontologist's leaving us alone a medical stratagem, or did he have a urinary infection? Had he gone to find a loudhailer so that he could walk up and down the hospital corridors shouting out that I had dementia? I don't live in Gray Lakes but you never know.

Five or so minutes later, the gerontologist returned sans loudhailer. Before sitting down, he planted both hands on his desk and leant forward so that he was looking down at me. From that position, he asked, 'How do you feel now?'

His voice was hard, his delivery harsh, and I wondered whether he was a member of a group of medicos who believed in talking tough to their patients no matter how vulnerable their patients might be. 'You don't have a hope in hell of lasting beyond Easter.' Shit happens.

Perhaps the whole Gray Lakes Medical Facility had a culture of ugly confrontation. Maybe the suburb of Gray Lakes did.

Marianne and I left. We were appalled. The gerontologist had made no projections. He had not looked to the future at all. His only further involvement was to stand close to his receptionist while she took six hundred dollars off me. His work was done. He had smoked another slacker out of a foxhole and ruined what remained of that slacker's pathetic life.

I was in shock for several days. And so was Marianne. Gradually, we began talking. Gradually, we began sharing our reactions. Gradually, we revisited what we could remember of that infernal test.

We went to see our GP. I spoke at length, head tilted, wild-eyed, babbling if the truth be told. Marianne intervened to slow me down, and to give her version.

Our GP listened, her face impassive. There was a pause. And then she spoke, 'Do you think you have dementia?'

'I have lapses of memory.'

'We all have those. They are symptoms related to ageing.'

A sense of joy began bubbling up inside me. 'All of us?' I said.

'Yes! We are all growing older and we all have age-related symptoms.' And in a magical moment she abandoned any temptation to have two bob each way, and said, 'Mike, you have been a patient of mine for more than ten years. You may have some age-related symptoms, but you do not have dementia.'

The next time I had lunch with that group of friends I told you about, I sat, biding my time until a moment offered itself and I chipped in and my good friends, my mates, burst out laughing.

I can't remember. Did I tell you I was eighty-one?

Old Friends

I want to say a little more about Dad.

Marianne, the kids and I touched down in Sydney mid-morning on 15 June 1982. I was there to take up my post at the Sydney Workers' Educational Association. Marianne and the kids were tagging along, and I had got them to do that much with the promise that we would return to the UK after three years if our move was not working out. We settled into my father's house on Sydney's north shore and immediately began looking for a house to purchase.

Dad died eighteen days later. And in those eighteen days, he went through a fascinating struggle…

He had been invited to replace the minister of the local Methodist church for three weeks and he had accepted immediately. 'It has given me an opportunity to heal some deep divisions in the congregation there,' he told me.

The differences emanated from the war in Vietnam, to which Australia had sent conscripts. Two extended families, all longstanding and active members of the church, had adopted radically different positions on the war and to Australia's involvement in it. One of the families had twin sons in their early twenties. With the support of their parents and other members of the family, the two sons became public draft dodgers, and when that became too difficult, they disappeared. The other family supported Australia's involvement in the war and they engaged in a relentless, wrathful condemnation of the twins and anyone else in the congregation who might have helped them.

'All this was more than eight years ago,' Dad said, 'but the bitterness is still there. I have three sermons to give and I am going to try to lay the basis for some kind of reconciliation.'

'Just the sermons?'

'No. Dialogue with the movers and shakers in each family. Various ruses to get some of the less outspoken to talk to each other.'

I must have looked sceptical because Dad cut our conversation off by saying, 'It's worth a try.'

Over the next fortnight, Marianne and I kept hunting for a suitable house. Dad withdrew into his study, emerging for meals, amiable as ever, but detached.

I did get him to talk once. His study door was not properly closed and I caught sight of him standing in the centre of the room with a book open in his hands. He looked up from the book and smiled. I pushed the door open and stepped into his study.

'How's it going?'

'More difficult than I thought.'

'Can I help? Do you want to try out some of the ideas with me?'

I looked at him and could see that he was considering my offer, but then he said, 'I think not. You don't know these people.'

'That's true,' I said, and withdrew.

The Sunday of the first sermon was fast approaching. Dad did not seem stressed but he had taken to locking himself in his study. We could hear the key turning.

At the end of another fruitless day of house hunting, we had a particularly joyful family meal. Dad was there. Yo and her two teenagers were there. Sandy, his partner, and his three kids were there. And of course, Marianne and I and our two were there.

While we were clearing up, Dad said to me, 'Come up to my study when you're finished here.'

I knocked on the study door. Dad ushered me in, and I could see a box of index cards on his desk. I knew the box well. The cards in it were a record of every sermon he had ever preached. Dad called the cards 'my old friends'. By keeping such a record, he could be sure that he never preached the same sermon in the same church twice.

I moved towards the desk.

'Yes,' Dad said. 'I'm looking through my old friends.'

'Which means…'

'I've abandoned my plan to restore peace and harmony to the local Methodist church. I just couldn't make a start.' He looked at me, momentarily bewildered, but it was followed by a gentle smile.

Mum used to be infuriated by Dad's gentle smile. 'How can he be so damn serene?' she would say.

Marianne and I found a suitable house shortly after Dad's death. I had wanted to spend longer living with Dad but that was not to be.

A very short love poem

My book is finished (and our revels now are ended).

One last thing. Most of the highlights I have described have been brief, but the most significant highlight of my life has been my marriage to Joelle Marianne Battestini, which, if you have been an attentive reader, you will know has been going on for well over fifty years.

In early 2003, Marianne was diagnosed with non-Hodgkin's lymphoma, and entered a six-year period of recurring attacks by the disease and recurring treatments by the medicos. These treatments included six courses of chemotherapy, two courses of radiotherapy and an autologous stem cell transplant.

Marianne fought back. She read extensively about the disease and its treatments, talked to other doctors and other patients, changed our diet radically, and engaged in a range of ancillary activities including yoga, meditation, psychotherapy and, when she felt up to it, walks in Centennial Park.

During a course of chemotherapy in 2009, the cancer went away. All of which leaves me with this inconsequential conundrum: was Marianne's confrontation with cancer a lowlight or a highlight? They were horrible, horrible years, but my partner in life emerged triumphant.

During the bad days, I was the carer, but during the periods of remission Marianne did her share of caring in return. How can I put this?

> I am suddenly awake
> Unsettled
> I reach out and touch you
> Your hand finds mine
> I sleep

And do not jump to the conclusion that Marianne's family name is Italian. It is Corsican.

Postscript

I finished writing this book and closed the lid of my laptop, only to be confronted by the news that a new disease was sweeping the land. I saw an aerial photo showing an improvised burial ground on an island in New York's Hudson River. Row upon row of white coffins. Bring out your dead. And why am I writing this? Ignoring Covid-19 would be impossible. At the very least, I must acknowledge that the world I have described in this book may never return.

Take care of yourself and others.

MN

www.ingramcontent.com/pod-product-compliance
Lightning Source LLC
Chambersburg PA
CBHW021056080526
44587CB00010B/266